AMERICA and
THE WILL of GOD

AMERICA and THE WILL of GOD

Religious Fanaticism, Democracy, and the Concept of God

Carlos A. Mojica

To order additional copies of this book, contact:
Xlibris Corporation
1-888-795-4274
www.Xlibris.com
Orders@Xlibris.com
41766

CONTENTS

To my dear sons, so that they never forget to use logical reasoning, never ignore history, and never underestimate the power of ignorance and superstition.

Preface

The election of George W. Bush in 2000 and 2004 brought into the American political forefront a group of voters that up to that point had remained somewhat in the margins, although not without influence. Evangelical Christians had made their political opinions known before, of course, with significant presence during the Reagan administration. In many past elections they had also donated sizeable amounts of money to particular political candidates, but with this President many of the issues they care about deeply seemed to come to the forefront of the national agenda.

Personally, I was baffled during the election campaign by the moral clarity and self-righteousness of the arguments against gay marriage, abortion, stem-cell research, Darwinian evolutionary theory, and other such "moral" issues. This President, at last a representative speaker for the evangelical Christians, had a clear vision of the right path to take on these complicated matters. The clarity came from his personal faith, straight from the Christian God. The Evangelicals were understandably energized. At last the possibility of a Christian United States could be at hand!

But hold on. Don't Evangelicals realize that theirs is not the only religion in America, and that there are other concepts of God out there with different mandates? Even more fundamental, the possibility that God does not exist is quite real, if one just goes through the trouble of thinking about it objectively. I do not question the strength of their faith, but I don't think Evangelicals realize that they could be wrong about everything! What is the truth regarding the concept of God? Does a strong faith create its own moral truths? Are any such "truths" universal and thus applicable to all, even non-Christians?

I am convinced that the concept of God is of human invention, but ultimately, as I hope I can demonstrate, the concept is irrelevant to the issue of personal morality and irrelevant to how our government must function. Yet, here are these people with crystal clear vision of right and wrong on exceedingly complicated and modern issues relying on judgments based solely on ancient religious thought, and personal faith. These voters are trying to impose their God-derived morality on everyone, along with visions of the United States that are anachronistic to our times and our history.

The belief in a particular God cannot be used as a basis to impose religiously derived moral values on others. Religious beliefs rest in faith, and faith ultimately rests on personal choice. To behave morally and hold particular beliefs all boils down to personal choice. However, the Evangelical answer appears to be: our faith is strong, our faith is true, "ours is a Christian nation", and as such our government not only cannot be secular, it has to be Christian! Thus the connection is clear; the Evangelical Christian God is the true God, His mandates encompass everything, and we need to change our country politically to represent His wishes. All this assumes, of course, that God really exists; but is this a reasonable assumption? Which God exactly, and who speaks truly on His behalf?

This book is an attempt to shake up those people on the fence that are, perhaps without realizing it, allowing our country to slowly be dominated by Christian conservatives. My strategy to accomplish this shakeup is quite simple. First, I critically examine the concept of God and show how there is an overwhelming probability that God is a figment of our imagination. I attempt to present, in the simplest of terms, some of the reasons why humans created the concept of God in the first place. I then argue that if in spite of the low probability of God's existence, one feels one must still believe in something, hopefully the reader will understand that accepting a particular concept of God is based on personal choice, not a fundamental and universal truth. By the end of the book I hope most readers will agree with my assertions that probably there is no God, and thus any derivation of any particular idea of "God" cannot and should not be imposed on anyone. As such, government, specially the one in America, must be secular if it is to remain a strong democracy.

I have traced a connection between the development of the concept of God and religion with historical and political forces as I understand them, and based my ideas on a purely personal appreciation of these. This book is not meant to be a strict historical treatise of religious development—there are volumes of such studies available—but instead I offer a broad-brush presentation of major historical forces and logical arguments highlighted and construed to make a point regarding religion in human affairs.

I do not add my voice to this discussion merely for the sake of attacking religion; I think people should be free to hold any beliefs they have (or should have) critically examined. What I am truly terrified of is the apparent turn towards fundamentalism in America, and how insidiously this movement is making its way into the political process. An apathetic and scared public appears to be standing by, like a deer startled by the oncoming headlights, unsure of what to do. When I bear witness to political machinery turning fundamentalist Christian (or Muslim for that matter), I see the institutionalization of ignorance, superstition, and bigotry. I indeed see a world gone mad.

I truly break little new ground in this ancient, oft-discussed subject. There exist vast collections of excellent books on this subject, available to any interested readers. The work by George H. Smith titled *Atheism—The Case Against God* stands in my view as definitive and conclusive in settling the question of why the belief in God is irrational; it is indeed a powerful exposition. In laying out my modest arguments, I have drawn extensively from this work as well as from the works of others.

It has taken me a long time to complete this modest work, as I have struggled with both the concrete reasons for doing so, and with the normal issues of writing. In the end, I've decided to finish the endeavor because I am truly concerned about what could happen in America if people do not speak out. I do not look favorably upon the possibility of a Christian theocracy in the United States. I do not see the placing of the Christian Ten Commandments in courtrooms as a positive development. I'm baffled by those passionately arguing against stem-cell research. I am appalled when Evangelicals see a silver lining in the chaos in Palestine, thinking Armageddon is at hand. I see madness when the United Nations is said to personalize the Antichrist. And I get terrified when millions of Americans seriously believe all of this. When I listen to people like Jerry Falwell, Pat Robertson, Ted Haggard, Keenan Roberts, and others, I shudder at the thought of people like them dominating our government. I do not know what else to do but exercise my vote and the privilege of setting my opinions on paper so that other Americans will think about these things as well. I have quoted many respected writers and thinkers throughout the book; I urge all my readers to read their books as well.

For the sake of simplicity throughout the text I have arbitrarily referred to God as male, although there is no reason to assume this entity is of any particular sex. I have also taken the position, admittedly subjective, that there is only one God, one Universal Creator, which all present-day religions presume to speak in behalf of. If in reality there is more than one God, (i.e. the Christians only talk to their God, which is a different entity to the Muslim God, which again is different to the Jewish God, etc.) I believe it would not change any of the arguments I present here.

In the course of finishing this book, Mr. Jerry Falwell suddenly died of a heart attack. I have decided to keep his quotations and my comments on them in the book as I believe Mr. Falwell's ideas are typical of others in the Christian evangelical community.

Lastly, in order to provide readers the maximum possibility for further investigation and cross reference, whenever I have felt the need to offer definitions of specific concepts, I have elected to use Internet sources. Specifically Wikipedia (the free on-line encyclopedia) has been used as a dictionary and for explanations or definitions on special topics, particularly philosophical ones. I have used Wikipedia, fully aware that the quotes might change over time, but I offer them to provide the most commonly understood explanation or definition on particular subjects available at the time of my writing. The topics are not specialized to a point where any reader would have difficulty finding more formally accepted definitions. Any biographical data in the reference section also comes from Wikipedia.

Biblical quotes are from the free on-line service www.biblegateway.com. In cross referencing these to the King James Bible, I have noted only minor and inconsequential differences.

Lastly I would like to thank my son Sergio for encouraging me to finish this enterprise, and to Ms. Beth Bruno for reading the complete manuscript and making many excellent suggestions.

1

Introduction—Frontal Attack on Secularism.

Anyone who cares about the fate of civilization would do well to recognize that the combination of great power and great stupidity is simply terrifying, even to one's friends.—Sam Harris in Letter to a Christian Nation.

I start writing this shortly after president George W. Bush begins his second term, at a time when American religious conservatives have found renewed political strength in the midst of discussion about "moral values". It seems the American religious Right now finally finds itself with the political capital to exercise its will on issues like abortion, gay marriage, stem-cell research, evolution, and allowing the Christian Ten Commandments in courtrooms. The future of a secular federal government seems to be in the balance. Both sides of our political spectrum are courting the fundamentalists in the hope of winning votes.

At the center of all these discussions around morality, the presumed "will of God" is implicit. This is so because the judgments regarding what is or is not "moral" are based on specific teachings presumed to come directly from the universal creator Himself. The President seems to reaffirm these viewpoints when he constantly reminds his listeners that ours is a "nation under God". The fact that humans have been unable to come to a consensus, not only on the identity of God Himself, but for millennia have debated and killed each other over the exact nature of God and His teachings, does not seem to come into play in the current discussion. To the American Christian Right, there seems to be complete certainty regarding who God is and what He wants from all of us; and they, more than anyone else, presumably know what that is.

Given that most people regard the honesty of politicians as questionable, at best, it may seem like a good idea to use expressed piety as a weather vane for personal and political character. It seems to be in vogue among politicians both on the Left and the Right to talk about, and make sure everyone knows, they believe in God. However, expressed religious piety does not guarantee that anyone, politician or otherwise, will act more honorably or more morally than a non-believing person. Demonstrated leadership, sense of history, personal honesty, intelligence, pragmatism amenable to compromise, candor, and an ability to express ideas clearly would seem to be better gauges for a successful presidency than expressions of religious piety.

It is interesting, and perhaps insightful to realize that a high degree of "moral clarity" appears to be a common feature among very pious humans of all religious persuasions. For example, no one can accuse Osama bin Laden of having anything less than complete faith and devotion to his God, and acting on what he considers to be God's teachings. From Osama bin Laden's point of view, his beliefs impart total lucidity to the fact that his stated mission is sanctioned by God Himself, and his followers get their strength to carry out their murderous enterprise by the power of their faith. In fact, the acts of September 11th have been called, not without some merit, one of the more successful "faith-based" initiatives in recent times (Sam Harris). Osama bin Laden is not the first person in human history to feel empowered by God to impose "moral values" on other infidels, not by a long shot (remember Tomas de Torquemada?). History is full of examples of deeply religious leaders, who are not only completely incompetent, but also capable of leading their flock to total ruin. The story of Jim Jones comes to mind [1]. This fact begs the millennia-old questions: On who's side is God? Who speaks truly on His behalf? How do we know?

Personally, the expressed religious piety of this particular President, combined as it is with other traits, such as intense stubbornness, utterly simplistic analysis of complex issues, and inability to articulate ideas clearly without crude one-liners strikes me as symptomatic of an underlying ignorant and superstitious nature. As such, I draw no comfort from it. That many Americans ecstatically embrace a change towards fundamental, literal Christian biblical dogma in our way of government is for me a worrisome development, and testament that we are at an important crossroads, having ultimately to make a decision between reason and secular democracy on one side, or the road towards a thinly veiled Christian theocracy on the other.

I do not want to imply that the American Christian right is in any way in the same league as Osama bin Laden, but I do believe they are driven to their political objectives by similar fundamental reasons—i.e. implementing their version of "the will of God".

The Bible teaches that civil government was God's idea (Romans 13:1). Since God created it, would he want his people to stay out of it? No. Jesus instructs: "Give to Caesar what is Caesar's and to God what is God's" (Matthew 22:21). Christ-followers are obligated to contribute to government, which in America means more than paying taxes. To abandon the political arena is to disobey Christ's command to be change-agents in our culture (Matthew 5:13-16). Christians have a biblical mandate to participate in government.—Kenyn M. Cureton [2]

"The mission of the Christian Coalition is simple," says Pat Robertson. It is "to mobilize Christians—one precinct at a time, one community at a time—until once again we are the head and not the tail, and at the top rather than the bottom of our political system." Robertson predicts that "the Christian Coalition will be the most powerful political force in America by the end of this decade." And, "We have enough votes to run this country . . . and when the people say, 'We've had enough,' we're going to take over!"—Pat Robertson [3]

Below Osama bin Laden's stated reasons for a call to Jihad. [4]

"We are seeking to incite the (Islamic) nation to rise up to liberate its land and to (conduct) jihad (holy war) for the sake of God."
—*Osama bin Laden as reported in* al-Jazeera, *June 1999.*

"I'm fighting so I can die a martyr and go to heaven to meet God. Our fight now is against the Americans."

—*Osama bin Laden,*
quoted by Al-Quds Al-Arabi *newspaper.*

"We—with God's help—call on every Muslim who believes in God and wishes to be rewarded to comply with God's order to kill the Americans and plunder their money wherever and whenever they find it. We also call on Muslim ulema, leaders, youths, and soldiers to launch the raid on Satan's U.S. troops and the devil's supporters allying with them, and to displace those who are behind them so that they may learn a lesson."

Feb. 1998—Bin Laden edict

"We should fully understand our religion. Fighting is a part of our religion and our Sharia [an Islamic legal code]. Those who love God and his Prophet and this religion cannot deny that. Whoever denies even a minor tenet of our religion commits the gravest sin in Islam." . . . *"Hostility toward America is a religious duty, and we hope to be rewarded for it by God . . . . I am confident that Muslims will be able to end the legend of the so-called superpower that is America.*

[Time Magazine]

From the story of Jim Jones, to the more recent suicide bomber incidents in the Middle East we have multiple modern-day examples of how religious beliefs can be transformed into extremism and fanaticism, and from there to complete madness. This same point is the main subject of Sam Harris' *The End of Faith*. The argument can be made that since it is through use of logic and reason that humans discover truths, once people have resigned the use of reason, no belief can be said to be "crazy". Indeed, fundamentalist Hal

Lindsey [5] assures us that many of the recent natural disasters, like hurricane *Katrina* for example, happened as direct punishment from God, and that the United Nations is under the influence of the Antichrist. Hal Lindsey said after hurricane *Katrina*:

> *It seems clear that the prophetic times I have been expecting for decades have finally arrived. And even worse, it appears that the judgment of America has begun. I warn continually that the Last Days lineup of world powers does not include anything resembling the United States of America. Instead, a revived Roman Empire in Europe is to rule the West, and then the world. [5]*

From the website advertisement for Lindsey's work titled *Great Global Deception* [6]:

> *The Antichrist Waits In The Wings. Very few realize how close we are to having our constitutional freedoms stripped away by the United Nations. For the first time at the recent UN Millennial Summit, the UN leaders came out with their design for a One-World-Government with blatant clarity. The cleverly worded UN Constitution will grant us freedoms—which it can take away—to replace freedoms guaranteed by the US Constitution that are granted by God and therefore irrevocable. Unless the message contained in this video is spread rapidly, Christians will find themselves on trial before a prejudiced and hostile world court for "the crime of saying that Faith in Jesus Christ is the only way to God and salvation."*

From the first passage we are to believe that God truly cares about Earth's geopolitics and which countries constitute some hypothetical and subjective "lineup of world powers". The implied message is that 'we need to do something aligned with Christian values or we are going to be on the wrong side of God's judgment', as in fact we have been already as proven (presumably) by the *Katrina* disaster. In the second he argues that God's antithesis, the evil antichrist, is personalized in the political organization of the United Nations whose real intention is to destroy America's *God given* constitutional freedoms. I believe Mr. Lindsay is one of a very few number of people who claim God Himself had something to do with the writing of the United States constitution. I leave to the reader any judgment regarding whether these opinions can be taken seriously or are to be considered those of a lunatic. In any case, Mr. Lindsay is vocalizing what he believes is God's prophesy, thus the "will of God" to his followers, and endorsing specific political action to avert disaster. Followers of Mr. Lindsay's ruminations would be wise to remember that *"Among all forms of mistake, prophesy is the most gratuitous"* (George Elliot).

Hal Lindsey's beliefs presumably afford him a clear God-given vision that America needs to implement Christian values and do away with the United Nations pronto, or else we will be punished severely. Osama bin Laden believes he is personalizing God's instructions to Muslims that they must stand guard and defend their religious values pronto, in order to stem the corruption of their culture. In addition, the United States must leave Saudi Arabia, Palestine and the rest of the Muslim world alone. It seems bin Laden's God is also concerned about Arab nations not being part of some "lineup of world powers"—God and twenty-first century geopolitics!

Americans are not alone in this modern religious revival, as events in Arab countries indicate. The new millennium, instead of ushering in an era of understanding and technology-based communication, seems to have brought us a revival of intolerance and a new wave of religious fanatics. Perhaps, technology-based communications only made fundamental culture incompatibilities too obvious to ignore for some people. In any case, the nature of God seems now to be discussed by fanatics in all corners of the world with renewed intensity.

Putting the basic question of the existence of a Universal Creator on hold for the moment, history has shown that when we bring God into the affairs of humans in the form of political actions, as the American Christian Right wants to do at present, things can get unnecessarily complicated and downright nasty. For instance, if gay marriage was being discussed solely in the context of the personal choice of fellow citizens and civil liberties, as opposed to whether or not it is morally forbidden by God, I doubt the issue would trigger the same passions as it brings out today in America. If you believe in the Christian God, why not let Him deal with the issue on an individual basis in the afterlife?

It is precisely because the Christian God as expressed in the Bible forbids homosexuality that Christians feel "marriage must be protected". Of course, the use of the word "protection" in this case is a vulgar euphemism for discrimination, as any serious attempt to truly protect marriage would involve making divorce illegal. After all, the Christian God also mandated: That which is brought together by God should not be dissolved by man. It is by way of misleading generalities such as "marriage must be protected" that the political Christian Right attempts to make a direct correlation between Christian-derived moralities and the way our government works, or between the presumed "will of God" and the laws of the United States.

As it happened in the last elections, American voters were swayed by clever political oversimplifications, like "standing for marriage and family" and for "a culture of life", euphemisms for being against gay marriage and against the right of women to choose ending their own pregnancy by having an abortion.

Right wing religious organizations have become intertwined with American politics to a disturbing degree, so that many evangelical churches and ministries now function as adjuncts of the Republican Party (or maybe visa versa). In 2004, ostensibly non-partisan ballot initiatives like Ohio's anti-gay marriage Issue 1 allowed churches to take over huge parts of the GOP's get-out-the-vote apparatus—they ran voter registration drives and massive phone-banking operations. Bush, in turn, has used the Faith-based initiative like a Tammany Hall patronage system to reward supportive religious leaders. Not all Republicans are part of the religious right, of course, but the movement has a huge degree of power in setting the party's agenda . . . . John McCain has learned this lesson well. In 2000, McCain tried to separate himself from the dominant block within the GOP, denouncing Pat Robertson and Jerry Falwell as "agents of intolerance." That kind of independence didn't work out too well for him, so this year McCain is embracing the forces he once disdained, giving the commencement speech at Falwell's Liberty University and telling Tim Russert, "I believe that the Christ—quote, 'Christian right,' has a major role to play in the Republican Party." Obviously, the history of American politics is filled with the deeply devout, but the emergence of a sectarian political party—one that frequently casts its opponents as not just wrong but metaphysically evil—is something new and ominous.—Michele Goldberg, Senior writer for Salon magazine [7].

Thus, the presumed will of the Christian God as expressed in the Bible is working its way into the American political and civil landscape. Our democratic process of elected government has resulted in a presidency empowered to "change government" to something that reflects the "Christian values" of his constituency. The Christian Right wants a Christian government, laws, judges, and a Congress that holds "Christian values". Evangelical Christians feel entitled to this because they feel they are in the majority (as expressed by the elections), and because they believe ours is in essence a country based on "Christian values". The argument that our government is supposed to work for *all* its citizens, gay, Muslims, Jewish, and atheists alike, is swept aside unceremoniously by evangelical Christians who feel our government has not worked for *them* for far too long.

> *"The Constitution of the United States, for instance, is a marvelous document for self-government by the Christian people. But the minute you turn the document into the hands of non-Christian people and atheistic people they can use it to destroy the very foundation of our society. And that's what's been happening."—Pat Robertson [8]*

It seems thus opportune that given the present religious revival in America, with its political agenda and moral clarity, that this is a good time to examine carefully the concept of God. I feel this is important because in our country, and indeed in all democracies, religion in all its different forms must be kept strictly separate from Government. Democratic governments, but particularly in America, must represent the values of all its citizens and work for the benefit of everyone; God, in all its manifestations, must be kept out of it.

Let us examine this concept of "God". I am not concerned merely with the Christian God as portrayed in the different denominations, or any particular God as presented by other religions, but the idea of God itself; the idea of a supreme, omnipotent, omnipresent, everlasting, all-knowing, most-masterful designer and creator of the infinite universe. I have often wondered what would happen if somehow it became known with total certainty that God and His spiritual realm do not really exist, and that death does indeed mark the end of one's existence in this or any other universe. Would humankind descend into complete anarchy? Would murderous chaos be inevitable? Would priests and ministers suddenly start robbing banks and raping children? Would judges become arbitrary autocrats and go into killing rampages? Would all human societal structures totally and inevitably collapse? Is this fate inescapable?

I do not believe so. I believe the vast majority of people would still try hard to obey the laws of the land, to get along with each other, and to make a better life for themselves and their loved ones. The belief in a God, shared it has been said by about 95% of the earth's population for most of recorded history, does not seem to have prevented humankind, including many people of faith, to commit horrendous crimes against fellow humans. History through the millennia is full of such examples. Thus religion alone cannot be argued to be an effective means of deterrence against war, chaos, severe cruelty, and inhumanity. So it does not follow that a world, or a country, composed mainly of atheists is bound to be immoral or destined to anarchy. As a matter of fact, the majority of the citizens in Sweden, Denmark, Norway, Japan, Finland, and France, countries which enjoy working democracies, living standards, and technological development comparable to ours, declare themselves to be either atheists or agnostics [9].

The concept of God has been recognized as a philosophical problem and debated as such for many years. Anyone with the slightest interest in this topic can find countless books on the debate and he or she will find that both sides have declared the case closed. Atheistic philosophers will lead those who study this question to the conclusion that the concept of God is irrational and a cruel figment of human imagination and superstition. Theists on the other hand will attempt to paint a subjective picture of some supernatural being-thing-force outside human understanding and stress the need to accept it on faith. But why is God needed? Particularly in a human institution concerned with the bureaucratic administration of a country? On a personal level, can humans not cohabitate peacefully, even morally, without the threat of God's eternal punishment? At the governmental level, can we not develop by ourselves the maturity to come up with government organizations and laws to make life bearable and fair for the sake of our own survival and peaceful coexistence? Why is this impossible without the intervention of some concept of God, or God-derived "moral values"? Do we need some God to accomplish the simple task of getting along and trying to forge a productive life? The traditional Christian answer through the ages has been; "We need God because human nature is weak and will eventually fall prey to sin". I think this argument is complete nonsense. It devalues the human intellect, it assumes we cannot assume responsibilities for our own actions, and it condemns us to a mythological idea where real progress is only obtained in response to celestial punishment.

I am convinced that for the whole of human history we have tried to do exactly what some think we need God's intervention for, i.e. making laws to make life bearable and fair for the sake of our own survival and peaceful coexistence, in many cases under the illusion of supernatural supervision, the make-believe rewards of heaven and the punishments of eternal damnation.

Humans, conscious of themselves but utterly alone, naked, scared, ignorant, confused, but possessing great imagination, created God both as a psychological crutch and as an explanation for the many uncertainties, calamities, mysteries, and wonders of life and the universe.

I do not pretend with my arguments to convince fundamentalist Christians to suddenly abandon their beliefs. I agree with those who consider that objective futile, most have resigned the use of reason and would be scared to even consider the idea of reading a book such as this one, to say nothing of a life without God. My modest objective is that my presentation of this topic will appeal to religious "moderates" to critically examine their reasons for religious beliefs and perhaps even reconsider these, or at least look at them in a different way. Hopefully, the examination itself, although perhaps not enough to make most abandon their beliefs, will at least make some realize the logic behind a strictly secular government and consider the validity of a moral code of behavior independent of any particular form of deity. I hope to help break some of the tenuous hold the Christian Right political machine has on the discussion about "moral values" by exposing how weak the concept of God really is, and how a moral code of behavior does not need any God to make sense.

2

Believe in God, But Which One?

Why does most of humankind believe in some form of supreme universal creator? Where did this idea of a supernatural and immortal being come from and is it relevant to how we ought to behave towards each other? More importantly, does God really exist? How do we know?

The concept of "God" and His relationship to the human species through the different organized religions is as much a part of the human experience as politics, sex, hunger, war, plagues, and love. Different from all of these, however, the concept of God and what He wants from us is not learned first-hand. The concept must be introduced to humans through religious dogma and comes wrapped in mystery and contradiction. Whatever God's intentions or desires are, they require translation and dissemination by special officials. God, in all His denominations throughout history and despite His enormous powers, has not openly and unequivocally made His presence and expectations known to all humans on a regular basis. He has not given us clear, widespread, and consistent instructions regarding our role in the universe, what to do, how to do it, or why. Every organized religion since the dawn of time has had a different set of rules and teachings from every other.

The question of God's existence is particularly relevant in America at present because time and again what are believed to be definitive conclusions derived from His teachings are placed as barriers to expanding what humans discover by experimentation or to prohibit how humans want to conduct themselves. This is not new; recorded history is full of examples from astronomy, through molecular biology, to anthropology where at some point God's teachings have been invoked as to why exploration in these areas was prohibited territory. The story of Giordano Bruno (1548-1600) who was burned at the stake by the Inquisition for theorizing about extra-solar planets and extra-terrestrial life is well known. The current "controversies" around Darwinian evolutionary theory and stem cell research, are just the more recent examples of this same phenomenon.

The reality is that the universal creator of the theists has been completely ineffective as a communicator. If He indeed exists, the fabulous work done creating the billion galaxies and the incredibly precise physical laws we see evidence of in nature has not been reproduced in securing a clear understanding and buy-in of objectives for the human species. In fact, religious wars caused by differences in interpretation of what some consider instructions left behind by God, or whose particular God is the "true" God, have been at the root of many of humankind's bloodiest and longest lasting conflicts. In the West, for example, take Protestants vs. Catholics, or Muslims vs. Christians, Jews and Christians. Aside from those who claim to have direct personal evidence of His existence, i.e. those who have spoken or heard Him through different revelations, for most theists believing in God is a matter of faith, not reason. Even more than that, for many people believing in God is a matter of *unquestionable* faith, but why? In the absence of tangible proof, is this unquestioned belief in an omnipotent God rooted in some mysterious insight intrinsic to humans, or is it the end result of several millennia of widespread religious indoctrination? Is this act of faith something reached after examination of all the data and serious adult reflection, or accepted as a matter of fact, implanted from early childhood and inseparable from family and culture? Are humans naturally designed to believe in God, or simply naturally superstitious? Are the current organized religions the conduit to understanding the mind of the universal creator, or the final evolution of an extremely intricate social structure that encompasses cultural, legal and political elements and that use human superstition and ignorance as their main tool for influence? The answers to these questions carry serious implications.

Personally, I am suspicious of anyone who states that God, Allah, or Jesus Christ speaks to him or her directly. Clinically speaking, there is no difference between hearing the voice of Jehovah or that of Napoleon Bonaparte. In any case, this selective communication is completely ineffective as an article of proof for the existence of the universal creator. Individuals are more than capable of self-delusion and of lying. If one is really hearing voices, the most logical explanation is that one is in need of professional psychotherapy.

Since before recorded history humankind has believed in supernatural beings. Early on most of these deities were direct answers to human ignorance. Before we knew about evaporation and condensation there was the God of rain who people thought could be favorably persuaded in times of drought by special dances. Before we knew about geologic plate tectonics there was the God of the volcano who lived in some mountain that erupted on occasion. The existence of gods not only offered explanations for our observations of nature, but also for natural disasters that early humans could not anticipate. In this case natural disasters were attributed to God's punishment. For example, in medieval Europe ignorant folk attributed all sorts of events, from the bubonic plague to bad crops, as specific punishments from their God. This tradition of connecting events with "the will of God" continues to this day. In the aftermath of hurricane *Katrina*, Pat Robertson suggested the storm was direct punishment on the United States because of the number of abortions done in this country. The conclusion being that in order to avoid future *Katrina's*, the practice must be abolished. Is this line of reasoning much different than the ancient practice of dancing to the God of the volcano to avoid disaster? The truth is, however, that Pat Robertson has another agenda behind this particular fear mongering:

> *You know, it's just amazing, though, that people say the litmus test for [Supreme Court nominee John G.] Roberts [Jr.] is whether or not he supports the wholesale slaughter of unborn children. We have killed over 40 million unborn babies in America. I was reading, yesterday, a book that was very interesting about what God has to say in the Old Testament about those who shed innocent blood. And he used the term that those who do this, "the land will vomit you out." That—you look at your—you look at the book of Leviticus and see what it says there. And the author of this said, "well 'vomit out' means you are not able to defend yourself." But have we found we are unable somehow to defend ourselves against some of the attacks that are coming against us, either by terrorists or now by natural disaster? Could they be connected in some way? And he goes down the list of the things that God says will cause a nation to lose its possession, and to be vomited out. And the amazing thing is, a judge has now got to say, "I will support the wholesale slaughter of innocent children" in order to get confirmed to the bench. And I am sure Judge Roberts is not going to say any such thing. But nevertheless, that's the litmus test that's being put on, the very thing that could endanger our nation [by inviting God's punishment]. And it's very interesting. Read the bible, read Leviticus, see what it says there—Pat Robertson. [1]*

In this example the connection between politics and the presumed "will of God" is direct and undeniable. That the benevolent creator of the universe, who presumably conjured physical laws with minute accuracy, would unleash such an indiscriminate and deadly wrath on innocent people in New Orleans and other cities cannot be explained convincingly. Here is another example:

> *(CNN)—Television evangelist Pat Robertson suggested Thursday that Israeli Prime Minister Ariel Sharon's stroke was divine retribution for the Israeli withdrawal from Gaza, which Robertson opposed. "He was*

dividing God's land, and I would say, 'Woe unto any prime minister of Israel who takes a similar course to appease the [European Union], the United Nations or the United States of America,'" Robertson told viewers of his long-running television show, "The 700 Club." "God says, 'This land belongs to me, and you'd better leave it alone,'" he said. [2]

The threat of God's punishment is never far away:

I'd like to say to the good citizens of Dover: if there is a disaster in your area, don't turn to God—you just rejected Him from your city. And don't wonder why He hasn't helped you when problems begin, if they begin. I'm not saying they will, if they do, just remember you just voted God out of your city. And if that's the case, don't ask for His help because He might not be there. [3]

Jerry Falwell provide us yet another example, this time on why America was attacked on September 11th:

"I do believe, as a theologian, based upon many Scriptures and particularly Proverbs 14:23, which says 'living by God's principles promotes a nation to greatness, violating those principles brings a nation to shame,'" he said.

Falwell said he believes the ACLU and other organizations "which have attempted to secularize America, have removed our nation from its relationship with Christ on which it was founded." "I therefore believe that that created an environment which possibly has caused God to lift the veil of protection which has allowed no one to attack America on our soil since 1812," he said. [4]

So in Pat Robertson and Jerry Falwell's universe, natural phenomena like hurricane Katrina, Ariel Sharon's stroke, or any future disaster on the city of Dover, Pennsylvania, plus unnatural acts like the terrorist attacks of September 11th, can be explained by explicit offenses against God. Neither Robertson nor Falwell explain why the universal creator did not punish specific sinful New Orleanians, ACLU members, or just gays and lesbians in the United States instead of bringing indiscriminate death to totally innocent people. Their God seems to be capricious and insensitive. What is the point of punishment if you do not even know what you are being punished for? The absurdity of the repugnant passages above to me is simple testimony of an amazingly ignorant, superstitious, and callous mind. That presumably millions of people seriously listen to what these men have to say is astounding and deeply worrisome.

But back to the concept of God. In addition to offering simple answers to natural phenomena, the concept of God has proven useful to deal with the ultimate mystery: Death. As stated by Charles Monroe:

> *Death is man's eternal enemy. Although intelligent humans know death is inevitable, most still hope that victory over death can be won in an afterlife of immortality. Man hopes to retain his hold on life by finding security or salvation from the many death-causing forces that surround him in his various environments. Man's struggle to maintain life has caused him, like the biblical Job to ask many questions: Why is man born into this world of struggle and death? Why must man be a victim of this cycle of life and death? How can I escape the terrors from the external and internal environments? What is life? How did creation happen?* [5]

The very first answers to all these questions, asked by all intelligent societies in every corner of the globe through millennia has been the same: **Gods!** Gods of every type, and all types of religious dogma. Anyone who has lost a loved one knows that death brings all of life into a clear and sobering perspective. We fear death, we fear what it means, we fear not knowing what, if anything, happens after we close our eyes that last time. We do not know what happens to our consciousness, and we obviously do not want to leave our loved ones behind. It seems the ultimate unfair irony that after a lifetime of hard work and investment in future concerns for ourselves and others, we all just simply and unceremoniously die. All of us will experience this.

You could die at any moment. You might not even live to see the end of this paragraph. Not only that, you will definitely die at some moment in the future. If being prepared for death entails knowing when and where it will happen, the odds are you will not be prepared. Not only are you bound to die and leave this world; you are bound to leave it in such a precipitate fashion that the present significance of anything—your relationships, your plans for the future, your hobbies, your possessions—will appear to have been totally illusory. While all such things, when projected across an indefinite future, seem to be acquisitions of a kind; death proves that they are nothing of the sort. When the stopper on this life is pulled by an unseen hand, there will have been, in the final reckoning, no acquisitions of anything at all . . . .

Without death, the influence of Faith-based religion would be unthinkable. Clearly, the fact of death is intolerable to us, and Faith is little more than the shadow cast by our hope for a better life beyond the grave. [Sam Harris, 6].

The ephemeral nature of life has been a topic of poetry and song, not to mention serious philosophical thought, for centuries. In *Life is Just a Dream*, Calderon de la Barca reminds us:

> *As life is longer than a summer's day,*
> *Believed himself a king upon his throne,*
> *And play'd at hazard with his fellows' lives,*
> *Who cheaply dream'd away their lives to him.*
> *The sailor dream'd of tossing on the flood:*
> *The soldier of his laurels grown in blood:*
> *The lover of the beauty that he knew*
> *Must yet dissolve to dusty residue:*
> *The merchant and the miser of his bags*
> *Of finger'd gold; the beggar of his rags:*
> *And all this stage of earth on which we seem*
> *Such busy actors, and the parts we play'd,*
> *Substantial as the shadow of a shade,*
> *And Dreaming but a dream within a dream!* [7]

The phenomenon of creating gods to explain the natural world has been loosely referred to as the "Gods of the Gaps" [8]. But, this act of creating gods out of gaps in our understanding has been recognized through the ages. For example, the early physician Hippocrates, of the famous Hippocratic oath, stated about 2500 years ago:

> *"People think that epilepsy is divine simply because they don't have any idea what causes epilepsy. But I believe that someday we will understand what causes epilepsy and at that moment, we will cease to believe that it's divine. And so it is with everything in the Universe".* [9]

We have also created gods that reflect human characteristics in complete totality except for the fact, of course, that all gods are immortal. The Greek and Roman gods, who experienced not only love but also jealousy, sexual desire, charity, and possessed unsurpassed speed, strength, and wisdom, are beautiful examples of this. Deities of every type have sprung forth in every human society that ever came to be in every corner of the planet. Anyone with the slightest interest in doing even a little research on this topic will discover the names of at least 61 Nordic Gods, about 20 Greco-Roman Gods, 18 Celtic, 15 native Irish, 13 native Welsh, 26 Slavic, 126 Japanese, and something like 200 African Gods [see Appendix 1], and all those are surely but a small sample when considering all human cultures since prehistory. Most people today, sophisticated as we think we are, would dismiss these old deities as ridiculous and would regard paying homage to them as completely nonsensical or even heretical. But during their time they were worshipped with as much faith and conviction as we offer our gods today. But, how does one really decide which God to worship? Is choosing a God a proposition based in logical reasoning? How do we come to decide which are "false" and which are "true" Gods?

Humans have thus created gods of every type from the very beginning; and these have served a variety of practical purposes: explaining natural and un-natural phenomena, and as a conduit to deal with death (which is also a natural phenomenon).

In very general terms, we can deduce that with the creation of Gods came other ideas and special institutions. For example, given the fact that none of our Gods, past or present, have communicated openly, directly or unequivocally with humans on a regular basis meant that some form of institution had to be created to translate, explain and disseminate whatever God's concerns were at any given moment. In the course of human affairs these necessities mark the creation of institutionalized religion and religious dogma. In addition, any idea of afterlife had to be accompanied by some description of what afterlife would be like. Not all religious concepts that have endured to this day have an associated element of afterlife, however, all Judeo-Christian derived religious denominations do. It follows that there have to be at least two forms of afterlife, one for good people, people we liked and who followed the teachings of the religious institution, and another for those who did not. It would make no sense that how one behaved in life towards others and towards the religious institution would have no bearing on your fate after death. Since religious institutions often became closely entangled with social and civic ones (in many cases they were one and the same) the rules derived to discriminate those going to the "good" afterlife from those not so fortunate incorporated both religious and civic elements. The main point is that the creation of the concept of God resulted in the creation of both religious and civic laws, and a moral code of behavior became synonymous with the idea of God itself—a perception that endures to this day.

Historically, this connection was not a bad development in itself as a legal system of justice, even a tyrannical one or one based on superstitious beliefs, ensures the peace of the tribe, and tribal peace is critical to the development of other civic institutions and of a working complex society. But in order for this system to work properly, everyone has to be part of the it, i.e. you could not opt out and there could not be alternative institutions; religious in particular. That different religious institutions eventually came into competition with each other has been at the root of many bloody conflicts among human cultures—this also continues to this day.

However, for those with a skeptical or critical view of things (philosophers and scientists primarily), there have always been several flies in the ointment. For example, ancient and current gods share the trait that inasmuch as they are "supernatural", humans simply can never begin to understand the basic nature of their God. That issue plus the fact that God is nowhere to be found are the underlying reasons for the need of religious faith (next chapter). Ultimately God itself is an abstraction that humans can never know directly; every particular God concept must be introduced and accepted on faith. Any concept of God is intrinsically mixed with the specific religious institution and the cultural underpinnings He sprung from, and the concept must be specifically taught, preferably since early childhood. Moreover, the religious institution has to be taken very seriously and cannot ever be challenged.

Take, for example, the Christian God that according to dogma created the visible and invisible universe about 6000 years ago. Such a God lies beyond the natural laws we observe in the universe and the laws He himself created, thus He is said to be "supernatural". The physical laws that govern us and all we see do not bind a "supernatural" being. As such, not only can God fly, but He also can travel through time, be everywhere at once, spontaneously create matter, know everything at once, speak to people in dreams, unleash hurricanes, inspire terrorist actions, etc. However, since humans can only understand natural laws, and this is difficult enough, a "supernatural" God lies beyond human comprehension. We cannot relate or begin to understand the how's and why's of a being which is not bound by the laws we understand. In this sense we will never really know the Christian God. In an attempt to describe God to believers the church puts out general descriptions. However, close examination reveals that what we get in the form of descriptions of the Judeo-Christian God are merely attributes of what constitutes being "supernatural": omnipotent, omnipresent, omnisapient, immortal, infinitely benevolent, etc. As rightly pointed out by G. H. Smith, that we can never know our God was even recognized by Saint Augustine:

> *What then brethren shall we say of God? For if thou hast been able to what though wouldest say, it is not God. If thou hast been able to comprehend it, thou hast comprehended something else instead of God. If thou hast been able to comprehend Him as thou thnikest, by so thinking thou hast deceived thyself. This then is not God, if thou hast comprehended it; but if this ise God, thou has not comprehended it.* [10]

The platitudes afforded to God are some of the same characteristics of any "supernatural" creature, but these really do not constitute a true knowledge of the nature of God. I submit to the reader that God is knowable to the same extent as other "supernatural" beings, like Santa Claus, Zeus, Apollo, or Superman. And is, just like these beings, a figment of a fertile imagination.

I draw several conclusions from these observations. First, left to our own devices in the face of a difficult problem, humanity's boundless imagination will make up for the lack of data, in this case the creation of a plethora of "Gods of the gaps". These Gods cover the complete span of human concerns, from hurricanes, terrorism, death, to metaphysical questions about life, our existence, and our purpose in this universe. Secondly, the concept of God is one that has proven particularly easy to conjure and easy to maintain because there is a lot more that we do not know than otherwise, and because a wise god/parent/king figure fits easily into the natural pattern of human family and societal structure. Third, the creation of religious dogma derived from the concept of God starts the process of the creation of laws that help maintain the peace of the tribe, and this positive development is attributed to God Himself. However, strength of conviction or numbers of converted does not equal validity of argument; thousands of people can be wrong or be mislead into wrong beliefs (e.g. there is a God of the volcano, the world is flat, the Sun revolves around the Earth, an UFO heaven flies hidden behind comet Hale-Bopp, drinking strychnine in the name of Jesus will not kill you, etc.).

Humankind's "Gods of gaps" phenomenon is revealing and should be examined carefully. If we accept the fact that the creation of "Gods of Gaps" is indeed part of the collective human experience—that creating gods is something we humans have done often and naturally, but that ultimately most if not all of these ancient gods, thousands of them since the beginning of recorded history and through the different cultures, are nothing more that a reflection of human imagination, triggered by ignorance, fear of death, and our need to understand—then we must be prepared to contemplate the possibility that the current accepted versions of deity are merely modern versions of the same phenomenon. Why should our current Gods, or other modern concepts of spirituality or afterlife, be any different or more justified to current believers than Quetzalcoatl, Ra, Thor, Aphrodite, Mercury, Chango, Azura Mazda, or countless others? Who made the determination that Jehovah is a better or truer god than Zeus and how was this conclusion reached? When it comes to faith and spirituality, is every idea equally valid? Or is this simply a numbers game; i.e. the more people share one particular God concept the more "correct" it is? Who made the determination that the God you worship is the "correct" one anyway? Are the differences between them relevant to the *concept* of God?

This is important, because given the lack of direct evidence for supporting one God over another, we really should either accept them all, or reject the whole concept. We must come to the realization that ultimately adhering to any particular religious faith is a matter of personal choice, one that has no more to do with logical reasoning than why my favorite color is blue.

The fact that humans have created thousands upon thousands of Gods strongly suggests that this popular idea belongs together with the human characteristic of creating stories. It makes perfect sense that humans would use their imaginations to solve both physical and metaphysical questions. To answer specific physical questions we have ultimately developed specialized scientific disciplines; to answer metaphysical ones we continue to rely on imaginary Gods and other concepts of afterlife and spirituality. Indeed the concept of God belongs in the realm of stories like those of mermaids, dragons, aliens from outer space, and superheroes. Moreover, it seems apparent that no concept of God or spirituality is really unique. There is no "one true God", in practical terms all are the same, and all pretty much accomplish the same thing: to explain some natural phenomena, which includes death, and set a moral code of behavior or philosophy about how to view this life and the next, the afterlife, where ultimate justice is dispensed.

In the span of all human experience we have devoted more of our imagination to creating and sustaining the idea of God or Gods, than to creating science or trying to get along better with one another. More to the point, there is no possible way to objectively discriminate one form of deity from another, other than your own cultural and historic background. There is no way to say Jehovah is better than Ra, who is better than Zeus, who is better than Vishnu, and so down the line. Nor can we say that the Bible is more the "word of God" than the Egyptians Book of the Dead, or the Koran (Sam Harris). The truth is that one is expected to assume the God of the tribe one is born into, and one is indoctrinated into believing in his or her particular God, and no other, by dogmatic policy, cultural pressures, and fear.

On this last point, both Christianity and Islam explicitly outline dire consequences for converting, disbelieving, ignoring, or cavorting with other faiths.

> *6 If your very own brother, or your son or daughter, or the wife you love, or your closest friend secretly entices you, saying, "Let us go and worship other gods" (gods that neither you nor your fathers have known, 7 gods of the peoples around you, whether near or far, from one end of the land to the other), 8 do not yield to him or listen to him. Show him no pity. Do not spare him or shield him. 9 You must certainly put him to death. Your hand must be the first in putting him to death, and then the hands of all the people. 10 Stone him to*

death, because he tried to turn you away from the LORD your God, who brought you out of Egypt, out of the land of slavery. 11 Then all Israel will hear and be afraid, and no one among you will do such an evil thing again.

12 If you hear it said about one of the towns the LORD your God is giving you to live in 13 that wicked men have arisen among you and have led the people of their town astray, saying, "Let us go and worship other gods" (gods you have not known), 14 then you must inquire, probe and investigate it thoroughly. And if it is true and it has been proved that this detestable thing has been done among you, 15 you must certainly put to the sword all who live in that town. Destroy it completely, both its people and its livestock. 16 Gather all the plunder of the town into the middle of the public square and completely burn the town and all its plunder as a whole burnt offering to the LORD your God. It is to remain a ruin forever, never to be rebuilt. 17 None of those condemned things shall be found in your hands, so that the LORD will turn from his fierce anger; he will show you mercy, have compassion on you, and increase your numbers, as he promised on oath to your forefathers, 18 because you obey the LORD your God, keeping all his commands that I am giving you today and doing what is right in his eyes. [Deuteronomy 13:6-18].

14 If anyone will not welcome you or listen to your words, shake the dust off your feet when you leave that home or town. 15 I tell you the truth, it will be more bearable for Sodom and Gomorrah on the day of judgment than for that town. [Matthew 10:14-15]

Jesus: 27 But those enemies of mine who did not want me to be king over them—bring them here and kill them in front of me." [Luke 19:27].

[Koran 2.126] And when Ibrahim said: My Lord, make it a secure town and provide its people with fruits, such of them as believe in Allah and the last day. He said: And whoever disbelieves, I will grant him enjoyment for a short while, then I will drive him to the chastisement of the fire; and it is an evil destination.

[Koran 3.12] Say to those who disbelieve: You shall be vanquished, and driven together to hell; and evil is the resting-place.

[Koran 3.19] Surely the (true) religion with Allah is Islam, and those to whom the Book had been given did not show opposition but after knowledge had come to them, out of envy among themselves; and whoever disbelieves in the communications of Allah then surely Allah is quick in reckoning.

[Koran 3.156] O you who believe! be not like those who disbelieve and say of their brethren when they travel in the earth or engage in fighting: Had they been with us, they would not have died and they would not have been slain; so Allah makes this to be an intense regret in their hearts; and Allah gives life and causes death and Allah sees what you do.

[Koran 5.86] And (as for) those who disbelieve and reject our communications, these are the companions of the flame. [i.e. Hell].

The historical record indicates that the concept of deity or faith we follow has more to do with when and where we are born than to any other factor with the possible exception of level of technological development and/or education. More importantly, we must not underestimate the effect in the collective human consciousness of centuries of effective religious indoctrination from early childhood. One that for centuries has touched on almost every aspect of human endeavor from political structures, the arts, early and late education, and one that has used fear—the fear of excommunication, or being burned at the stake, of forced exile, and of eternal damnation in afterlife—as effective tools to keep people in line plus dissent and dissidents to a minimum. The human psyche is not as robust as one might think, nor do humans as a collective always examine ideas critically, especially one as popular as this one. It takes only the first few bars of Bach's St. Matthews Passion to stir even the most ardent atheist into a bit of doubt; use this same tool on the illiterate masses at Westminster Abbey or the Toledo Cathedral, add some passionate oratory on fire and brimstone, have all your political structures and most of the social ones wrapped under the same veil, then finally control the development and dissemination of science and the scientific method, and the effects will last centuries, guaranteed.

This is indeed what has happened. Particularly in the West, different forms of Christian denominations (from Roman and Orthodox Catholic through all the protestant denominations) have been either intimately involved or critically influential in politics (from appointing kings to launching religious wars), in the arts (sacred music, paintings, sculptures, and architectural undertakings), and in education (from elementary school through university) since the end of the Roman empire through the present day. Thus, it is fair to contemplate the argument that given the overreaching importance and influence that religion has had in human affairs, when it comes to the subject of God, it is extremely difficult for individuals to be objective or detached. Many of our religious ideas, feelings, and beliefs have been implanted by an inseparable amalgam of political and social institutions, culture, community, and family, plus well cemented by the use of psychology, fear, and repression.

Let me offer an example to illustrate this last point. I think most people today would disregard any warnings from anyone claiming he or she had experienced a revelation from the God Solrac which claimed that unless the rest of us immediately claimed Him as the one true God, we would face total global annihilation of biblical proportions without notice. The warning would be specific in that people would be taken directly to Hell in physical form (not spiritual form) and with a very short time to leave, and that only those believers in Solrac as the true savior would be spared. Would we consider the bearer of such prophesy as one out of touch with reality, seriously delusional, or even downright crazy?

Now, exchange Solrac for Jesus Christ and it suddenly sounds familiar. Indeed, what I'm describing above is exactly what Christians believe will happen in the end-of-times Rapture [see 11]. The only reason we are even willing to extend the courtesy of a wide open public forum and to treat with dignified respect people with just these same wacky ideas of the universe is that we've all grown up with this particular mythology. Is an accepted view of what is probable, even though under any other circumstance we would demand some form of verification or data. In this particular instance, and just this one, many of us believe it on faith, no questions asked. We have all been subjected to indoctrination. Why is this revelation any less believable than Heaven's Gate prophesy of Heaven behind comet Halley-Bopp?

Serious rejection of religious ideas comes only after a process similar to detoxification, involving years of independent study and not without a fair amount of guilt, self-doubt, societal scowl, and individual rejection.

In conclusion, the concept of God has been part of the human psyche since humans became humans and is a natural byproduct of our imagination. The concept is singularly potent for many reasons, but paramount among these the concept of God helps explain natural phenomena, offers a way to cheat or explain death by providing for the possibility of an afterlife, and it offers different forms of psychological solace. The development of the concept of God also had the unintended consequence of helping create a moral code of behavior partly to go along with the concept of afterlife. This is so because it does not seem fair that person A, who was by all accounts a good guy, will end up after death in the same nice place that person B, a real bastard, will end up. Nevertheless all our Gods, thousands of them since the dawn of time, did not come to us in cosmic revelations or from holy books, *we invented them.* We invented Zeus, we invented Ra, Quetzalcoatl, Mercury, Chango, Poseidon, Thor, Neptune, Vishnu, Jehovah, Aphrodite, and countless upon countless others. Not only did we invent the creature itself, the actual image of either a bearded man or a multi-armed woman, we invented all the political and community structures that support it. All of it is the result of our fertile imagination. All our Gods are the same invention repeated tribe after tribe and time after time. Imposed and enforced by the religious institutions we ourselves created. Ultimately however, we must realize that conceptually if one of them is a false God, then all of them are because they are all the same invention. We must conclude that the concept of God is a common figment of our collective imagination.

3

Science and This Thing Called Faith.

'I have found it necessary to deny knowledge, in order to make room for Faith'. Immanuel Kant [1]

An interesting aspect related to the "Gods of Gaps" phenomenon, spills over to the on going "debate" between science and religion. For example, some religious people find arrogant the proposition that "everything in nature can be explained by science" and point to the many breaches in scientific understanding as argument that since complete scientific explanations are impossible, then "logical" reasoning inescapably leads to the conclusion that "there must be a God". At its core, this line of reasoning is indeed the basis for the whole "Intelligent Design" movement. The following quotes are typical:

> *. . . I cannot conceive of a man endowed with intellect, perceiving the ordered universe about him, the glory of a mountain top, the plumage of a tropical bird, the intricate complexity of a protein molecule, the utter and unchanging perfection of a salt crystal, who can deny the existence of some higher power."—Astronaut Scott Carpenter* [2].
>
> *How can we decide whether Darwinian natural selection can account for the amazing complexity that exists at the molecular level? . . . . Some systems seem very difficult to form by such successive modifications—I call them irreducibly complex . . . [an] example of*

irreducible complexity is the system that allows proteins to reach the appropriate subcellular compartments. In the eukaryotic cell there are a number of places where specialized tasks, such as digestion of nutrients and excretion of wastes, take place. Proteins are synthesized outside these compartments and can reach their proper destinations only with the help of "signal" chemicals that turn other reactions on and off at the appropriate times. This constant, regulated traffic flow in the cell comprises another remarkably complex, irreducible system. All parts must function in synchrony or the system breaks down. Still another example is the exquisitely coordinated mechanism that causes blood to clot." Michael Behe [3]

Given that humans have been studying nature in an organized way for only something like 300 years (~10 generations) we should have no problem coming to grips with the idea that humans do not understand everything. But is "understanding everything" a reasonable objective and absolute prerequisite to finally questioning the existence of a universal creator? Can science ever explain everything and is this how the question of God is ultimately going to be settled? Does incomplete knowledge equal proof of Gods existence? Is this leap from "this is too complex" to "there is a God" a reasonable one?

Carefully examined, this argument is nonsense. As others have pointed out, this position rests on equating knowledge and certainty, with infallibility (G. H. Smith). In reality, humans have no one to help us in acquiring knowledge, so the process is slow, mistakes are made, and the process is far from perfect:

> *. . . man has to acquire knowledge by his own efforts, which he may exercise or not, and by a process of reason, which he may apply correctly or not. Nature gives him no automatic guarantee of his mental efficacy; he is capable of error, or evasion, or psychological distortion. He needs a method of cognition, which he himself has to discover: He must discover how to use his rational faculty, how to validate his conclusions, how to distinguish truth from falsehood, how to set criteria of what he may accept as knowledge.—Ayn Rand* [4]

Absent from the above quote by Ayn Rand is God. As it happens, neither God, nor the Bible nor the Koran nor any other holy book, can be counted on to help humans gather knowledge.

The most reliable method humans have devised to acquire knowledge is the scientific method. We must understand that *Science* in this context is more a deductive method than a specific discipline. The basic scientific method to gain knowledge is very simple and has been laid down on paper formally since the time of Francis Bacon (1561-1626), but surely it was used well before then. It very simply consists of first formulating a theory and second verifying or discarding it based on observable facts or direct experimentation. It has been the primary tool humans, the ignorant lonely creatures that dwelled in caves, developed to come up with verifiable truths. However, by its own nature the scientific method is an evolutionary process where degrees of understanding are reached by a slow method of developing ideas and actively testing them. What is important to realize is that the process *never ends*. It never ends because there always will be another question to be asked, some aspect not completely understood, some relationship that needs fine-tuning, or because sometimes data can be interpreted in different, even opposing, ways. However, the fact that there always will be some gap in our understanding of the universe cannot serve as proof of the existence of an omnipotent Creator. This is simply another variant of the "God of gaps" phenomenon. Those that sort through all the controversies around evolution, cell biology and other scientific disciplines and ultimately point out the different interpretations, contentious results, and apparent inconsistencies as proof that creation is too complex for random chance (mutations, blood clotting, etc.) and conclude therefore that the existence of God (or some "intelligent designer") is the only plausible solution, are right in step with the "God of gaps" tradition. The concept of God is not an alternative theory to understanding the universe, God is a complete explanation to all problems; a solution that does not allow any competition as any inconsistency can be explained simply as "the will of God" or a miracle. Especially since, as already presented, a "supernatural" God presupposes a being not bound by the laws of nature.

The concept of God is one that cannot be either proven or refuted as there is no data to examine and it principally stands on faith. Fundamentally there is no difference between *"I do not understand why the volcano erupts, therefore there must be a God"* and *"Science cannot seem to explain how exactly primates became humans, or why the protein molecule and blood clotting are so beautifully complex, therefore there must be a God"*. Proof of the existence of the supreme creator cannot rely on the fact that there are gaps in our understanding of nature because one cannot use lack of data to support the very idea one is trying to prove. There is no direct irrefutable data or evidence for the existence of God except presumably "incomplete" data on the other side. There is no deductive connection between "I don't know" to "there is a God", because by coming up with God as an explanation one has in effect made up the answer. In fact, "because God made it so" is probably the oldest and most primal answer in humankind.

Moreover, that some feel current scientific explanations of observed natural processes are "too complex" to happen by chance (evolution, blood clotting, etc.) is essentially a completely arbitrary personal viewpoint with as much validity as disliking the New York Yankees. Why does the physical world have to conform to any particular contemporary human perspective of complexity or "beauty"?

This argument is often confounded with a populist notion of statistical probability; i.e. chance alone cannot explain very high degrees of complexity (the "irreducibly complex" argument used by proponents of Intelligent Design). The example of comparing present natural processes or biological systems with the probability of a hurricane constructing a Boeing 747 purely by chance is often brought up in this context. Proponents of this argument appeal to a general sense of what appears reasonable; surely the chance construction of an airplane purely by serendipity is absurd. But this is not what evolution is about. The emptiness of the irreducibly complex argument, has been well documented elsewhere (for example in David Mills *Atheist Universe—Why God didn't Have a Thing With It)*. This argument is vacuous primarily in that it misrepresents Darwinian evolutionary theory. In any case, theists should tread carefully when bringing in the concept of probability, particularly when discussing how the universe and life in this planet came about. If we are going to appeal to a populist notion of probability, then we all can play the game. For example, what is more probable, an abracadabra presto-pronto genesis by a cosmic magician who then disappears leaving behind no evidence? Or a slow evolutionary process, evidence of which we can find everywhere in the fossil and geologic record?

Darwinian evolutionary theory does not support the notion of magical and spontaneous generation of a fully developed biological or biochemical process. Darwinian evolutionary theory rests on the fact that systems evolved precisely from the simple to the complex in a stepwise manner given the imperatives of survival of the fittest and successful mutations over the course of millions of years. But this is well known (or should be) by proponents of Intelligent Design. The only conclusion one can draw from this obvious misrepresentation is that it is meant to muddle the true state of affairs regarding evolutionary theory and mislead the uninformed public.

In any case, I can agree that nature, or some aspects in nature appear to me as incredibly beautiful and maddenly complex, but taking this personal appreciation as testament for the existence of God is a stretch bordering on mystical poetry, not a discovery of a fundamental truth. Complexity cannot serve as the fingerprint for the universal creator because the concept of complexity is subjective. Statistical improbability, like the serendipitous construction of airplanes in scrap yards, is not what Darwinian evolutionary theory is proposing.

The theists really want it both ways. When complex natural phenomena are explained by scientific and not metaphysical arguments, we are told we are "discovering the mind" of the creator (in jest? by Stephen Hawkins); yet when the phenomena appear to be too complex or beautiful and science renders an "incomplete" answer, then we are told this is evidence of the existence of the creator.

> *Faith* [or the belief in an intelligent designer] *is required only if reason is inadequate; if reason is not deficient in some respect, the concept of faith becomes vacuous. The Christian creates the need for faith by denying the efficacy of reason. Without the element of denial, faith is stripped of its function; there are no gaps of knowledge for it to fill.—G. H. Smith* [5]
> *The way to see by faith, is to shut the eye of reason. (B. Franklin)*

Ignorance, i.e. "we do not know the answer", might be a very poor proof for God's existence, but is a completely reasonable, albeit unsatisfactory, state of affairs for humans and scientists given how we acquire verifiable knowledge.

For most of human history we have been ignorant about many aspects of the world around us. However, it is only through the use of the scientific method that we have acquired whatever understanding of the universe we possess now; and it is only through the scientific method that we will get any satisfactory answers. Religion and the belief in God rely first, foremost, and exclusively on faith; by definition there is no proof, no substantive data to examine. Relying on any form of religious "revelations" (from the Bible to near-death experiences) to attempt to understand the nature of the universe or to answer questions such as, How old is the Earth?, Why does it revolve around the Sun?, Why is the Sun hot? Did humans evolved from primates? is paramount to calling the Psychic Hotline and expecting reliable answers. Explanations for very old and highly specialized natural, chemical, biological and physical processes are bound to be complicated, i.e. the true answers to complicated questions are bound to be complicated. And humans will naturally feel awestruck by their discoveries and by the complexity of these systems. But "complexity" is no reason to conjure some concept of God.

The inadequacy of equating "complexity" with a logical proof for the existence of the universal creator can be quickly realized when one considers a hypothetical scenario involving the Space Shuttle. Imagine for a second that by some technological breakthrough we could send the Space Shuttle back to the 1770s—with no explanation whatsoever. It follows that scientists pouring over the technology represented in the Space Shuttle would be completely blown away with what they found. They would be amazed at the variety of electrical devices, computer technology, different types of engines, sensors, and so on. In fact, the gap in what the scientists of the 1770s understood of nature and what they would see in front of them would be simply unfathomable. To paraphrase Arthur C. Clarke: The technical achievements and mechanical trinkets of highly advanced civilizations would be indistinguishable from magic. Not knowing where it came from and ignorant about what they were seeing, would some people in 1770 consider the Space Shuttle the creation of God (or maybe the Devil)? How about non-scientific lay people: Would they see proof of God in a flying *Space Shuttle* weighing several tons? In this example, those who saw the work of God would have failed to realize that what they were witnessing was the end result of years of focused airplane evolution, which began with a glider made out of canvas and a wooden frame.

If today we were to meet creatures from other planets that are ten times smarter than we are, thousands of years more advanced technologically, able to live 500 Earth-years, and able to travel light-years in seconds, would we consider them *de-facto* Gods compared to us? Humanity has encountered similar, although not so dramatic, circumstances before. The Aztecs and other native Indians in the Caribbean first thought the Spanish Conquistadors were Gods. One can almost imagine some of their leaders commenting on the glory of their sails and the *irreducible complexity* of their vessels' running rigging (take one piece out and the whole thing collapses!) and accepting these as testament to the Spaniard's deity. Only time and close observation convinced them otherwise.

My main point is that complexity by itself is a malleable concept; it depends on one's specific status and thus offers a poor proof for the existence of God. A concept of "complexity" that ignores evolutionary theory does not equal design, nor does it prove that there is a designer. The concept of complexity in this context is a corollary to human feelings of awe and is the result of insight into new discoveries.

There are some scientists that feel uncomfortable with the obvious conflict between science and religion. Some advance the proposition that:

> "*Science in no way argues against the existence of God, or Being, and can profoundly augment the sense of the cosmos as a significant whole*"—*Robert Nadeau and Menas Kafatos*, [6].

Although the statement above is true in the sense that the physical sciences, which rely on data and experimentation, cannot stand in the way of something unprovable and unknowable, it seems more conciliatory than insightful. However, it is ultimately nonsense. Science may not be incompatible with religion, but it is certainly incompatible with superstition (Ann Druyan), and explaining this distinction soon leads to the slippery road of incongruities. The crux of the incompatibility is the issue of faith, and conciliatory scientists notwithstanding, religious leaders through the centuries have been correct in being concerned about the conflict between reason and faith (i.e. science and religion) because the rift is real and irreconcilable. So yes, perhaps science has nothing to say if a consenting adult decides on faith to believe in the existence of the Supreme God of the Volcano, but it will certainly have something to say if the God presupposes an explanation for why the volcano erupts. In any case, supporters of such theistic beliefs have essentially decided to embrace superstition and scientists have allowed them to do so. Any augmentation of some "*sense of the cosmos as a significant whole*" is neither a true endorsement of religion, nor a scientific observation; it is simply poetry.

Theist scientists represent a special conundrum when it comes to the question of God. A theist reader might argue, *"If the concept of God is so irrational, why do so many scientists believe in God? Is this not a contradiction?"*

The case of Albert Einstein is often brought up in this context. Albert Einstein did indeed believe in the existence of God. His concept of God, however, was very individual.

> *Certain it is that a conviction, akin to religious feeling, of the rationality and intelligibility of the world lies behind all scientific work of a higher order. The firm belief, which is bound up with deep feeling, in a superior mind revealing himself in the world of experience, represents my conception of God, which may, therefore be described in common parlance as 'pantheistic'.* [7]
>
> *Pantheism—It is the view that everything is of an all-encompassing immanent God; or that the universe, or nature, and God are equivalent. More detailed definitions tend to emphasize the idea that natural law, existence, and the universe (the sum total of all that is, was, and shall be) is represented or personified in the theological principle of 'God'.* [8]

Einstein rejected the medieval concept of the Christian God. He also discarded most religious dogma. Superstition and the form of God professed by Osama bin Laden and Jerry Falwell would have repulsed him.

> *I cannot imagine a God who rewards and punishes the objects of his creation, whose purposes are modeled after our own—a God, in short, who is a reflection of human frailty. Neither can I believe that the individual survives the death of his body, although feeble souls harbor such thought through fear or ridiculous egotisms.* [9]

He was a spiritual man in the sense that having had a peek at the complexity of the universe, he felt dumbfounded and insignificant, and concluded that some universal designer was evident in this mathematical order.

It was, of course, a lie what you read about my religious convictions, a lie which is being systematically repeated. I do not believe in a personal God and I have never denied this but have expressed it clearly. If something is in me which can be called religious then it is the unbounded admiration for the structure of the world so far as our science can reveal it. [10]

Nevertheless, he had a spiritual side:

Science can only be created by those who are thoroughly imbued with the aspiration toward truth and understanding. This source of feeling, however, springs from the sphere of religion. To this there also belongs the faith in the possibility that the regulations valid for the world of existence are rational, that is, comprehensible to reason. I cannot conceive of a genuine scientist without that profound faith. The situation may be expressed by an image: science without religion is lame, religion without science is blind. [11]

Einstein seems to suggest in this last passage that in reality scientists can only hope that the laws of nature can be comprehended by the likes of us (thus rational), and that these apply everywhere the same way. He equates this hope with the concept of faith, and argues that this hope/faith *springs from the sphere of religion*, i.e. is a philosophical argument.

I believe the reader would agree Einstein's "religiosity" is not mainstream dogmatic religion. However, it is true that many scientists today adhere to this sentiment of Pantheism; i.e. God = Nature.

Like most human beings—surely those who use their full mental capacity—Einstein pondered long and hard on the question of God. His work on theoretical physics, where scientists are really trying to decipher the physical laws obeyed by both atoms and galaxies, led him to the default posture that there must be some "cosmic intelligence", as he himself called it.

Although I am a typical loner in daily life, my consciousness of belonging to the invisible community of those who strive for truth, beauty, and justice has preserved me from feeling isolated. The most beautiful and deepest experience a man can have is the sense of the mysterious. It is the underlying principle of religion as well as all serious endeavor in art and science. He who never had this experience seems to me, if not dead, then at least blind. To sense that behind anything that can be experienced there is something that our mind cannot grasp and whose beauty and sublimity reaches us only indirectly and as a feeble reflection, this is religiousness. In this sense I am religious. To me it suffices to wonder at these secrets and to attempt humbly to grasp with my mind a mere image of the lofty structure of all that is there. [12]

It seems clear to me that Einstein's concept of God is a reflection of the deep respect and admiration he had for nature and the universal physical laws, some of which he himself discovered. In simple terms, Einstein is describing a feeling of awe derived from a particular insight (some theists might even call this a "revelation"—though I would like to point out that faith is not needed to verify general relativity). It seems obvious to me that this perspective came as a natural byproduct of the work he was undertaking in theoretical physics and the remarkable discoveries he was making. However, and perhaps more pertinent to our discussion, Einstein's cosmic intelligence does not demand worship from humans, nor does it impose a specific moral code of behavior. There is no dogma associated with Einstein's pantheistic God. Although he denied it, it is really a personal God in the sense that only Einstein himself knew exactly what he was talking about. Others may agree with him on philosophical points, or agree he was perhaps into something perceptive or insightful, but it is still mainly a personal appreciation. In any case, Einstein's God does not pretend to impose its will or Christian values on humans, nor would Einstein have supported the formation of a Christian nation or teaching intelligent design in biology class. Whether Einstein's vision of God is another variant of the God of Abraham, is a matter of faith and personal perspective.

In a more general sense, scientists are, it is presumed, individuals who have not only embraced the scientific method as a means to acquire knowledge, but have been trained to be skeptical and critical of unsubstantiated claims about the nature of the universe. Indeed, the authors of a 1998 study published in the scientific journal *Nature* state that:

> *The question of religious belief among US scientists has been debated since early in the century. Our latest survey finds that, among the top natural scientists, disbelief is greater than ever—almost total.* [13]

So the perception that the majority of scientists are theists is perhaps a misconception. It seems a reasonable assumption that scientists as a population are indeed more atheistic than the population at large, where the numbers in the United States have hovered around 10% on the last few decades [14]. Whatever the numbers are, the apparent contradiction a theist scientist represents presupposes that 100% of scientists can transpose specific training in some scientific discipline, say biochemistry, from physical problems encountered in the workplace or laboratory, to metaphysical and philosophical preoccupations pondered during their leisure time or during some life event. Scientists, like all other humans, can just as easily compartmentalize and separate job from personal preoccupations, plus they also are as susceptible to religious indoctrination and mental evasion as the rest of us. Or, just as well as anyone else, they can invent their own personal concepts of deity or religiosity, thus wandering into the realm of religious philosophy. Ultimately, however, faith must come into the picture.

The conflict between reason and faith-based religious beliefs, like many other aspects concerning the concept of God, has been recognized for many years.

> *. . . discussions in favor of faith are always accompanied by references to the limits of reason. The Christian must use this procedure in order to prepare the necessary groundwork for faith . . . . The Christian who postures as an advocate of reason is often quite subtle in his attack on reason. Yes, he says, reason provides man with knowledge of reality; yes, reason is vital to man's existence; yes, man's rational capacity is his distinguishing characteristic—but some aspects of existence cannot be comprehended by*

man. Some facts are closed to rational understanding. Reason is fine as far as it goes, but it is limited. And here faith makes its grand entrance. Faith is called upon where reason is said to fail, and faith is represented as a supplement to reason, not an enemy.—G. H. Smith, [15]

We are all free to believe whatever we want to believe, but the truth is that there is a body of knowledge that humans have verified through a variety of methods and thus can accept as certifiably real, consistent, dependable, and predictable; and other beliefs, religious ones in particular, which are not. The concept of God, which ultimately rests on faith, is not one of the former. Accepting something on faith is, by definition, accepting a belief in the absence of any tangible data. *"The assurance of things hoped for, the conviction of things not seen"* [Hebrews 11:1]. Even Einstein's pantheistic God requires faith. His perspective may sound like a plausible, more realistic, perhaps a more modern or acceptable description of God (perhaps an improvement over the traditional Judeo-Christian one), but the conclusion that it is a manifestation of reality is based on a personal perspective, a hunch—on faith—and is not something provable.

> *. . . Faith is nothing more than a willingness to await the evidence—be it the Day of Judgment or some other downpour of corroboration. It is the search of knowledge on the installment plan: believe now, live an un-testable hypothesis until your dying day, and you will discover that you were right.—Sam Harris* [16].

Sam Harris goes on to say:

> *In any other sphere of life, a belief is a check that everyone insists upon cashing this side of the grave: the engineer says the bridge will hold, the doctor says the infection is resistant to penicillin—these people have defensible reasons for their claims about the way the world is. The mullah, the priest, and the rabbi do not . . . . How does the mullah know that the Koran is the verbatim word of God? The only answer to be given in any language that does not make a mockery of the word "know" is—he doesn't.*

By which he means the mullah takes on faith that the Koran represents the word of God. However, faith is an inadequate refuge for the theist:

If we cannot understand the concept of God, we do not come closer to understanding it through faith. If the doctrines of Christianity are absurd, they do not lose their absurdity through faith. If there are no reasons to believe in Christianity, we do not gain reasons through faith. Faith does not erase contradictions and absurdities; it merely allows one to believe in spite of contradictions and absurdities.—G. H. Smith [17]

Putting aside for the moment the fact that the scientific method is the only real tool we have to derive reliable explanations of the universe, adherence to it means that you appreciate in full knowledge of the facts that there will always be gaps. One is not accepting anything on faith, or because it feels "right" at some gut level. Ultimately it boils down to religion and God being one answer to ignorance, a conclusion based on blind acceptance and by design total and complete; the other being realization that there will be levels of understanding that we will have to accept, and enduring the process to bridge the gap in small, neverending, but verifiable steps. If as a species we really are going to learn anything about how the universe works, it will have to be by the use of the scientific method. Religion by itself is static. It does not evolve; it does not acquire new insights; it is set in dogma handed down by selected individuals' interpretations of old ideas and manuscripts. God Himself, if He is out there somewhere, is, of course, of no help whatsoever.

With science you are going in with full knowledge of the difficult task ahead and tackling the problem head on; with religion you are giving up and coming up with your own answer. In fact, theism, by endorsing a doctrine in complete opposition to the only tool humans have to acquire knowledge and by insisting on an irrational belief of the unknowable, actually insults human intelligence.

> *Theism represents an attack on man's ability to understand the universe,*
> *and the advocacy of theism, theology, attempts to reduce man to a state*
> *of perpetual ignorance. The concept of god, as Spinoza put it, is an*
> *asylum of ignorance. G. H. Smith* [18]

As far as faith is concerned:

> *Insofar as faith is possible, it is irrational; insofar as faith is rational, it*
> *is impossible . . . This dilemma is a consequence of the fact that reason*
> *and faith cannot simultaneously be offered as grounds for belief. A belief*
> *can be based on reason or faith, but not both. This makes it impossible*
> *for the Christian to maintain the rationality of faith because as soon as*
> *a belief is rationally demonstrated, it ceases to be an article of faith. This*
> *is the essence of faith: to consider an idea as true even though it cannot*
> *meet the test of truth, to consider an idea as having a reference in reality*
> *while rejecting the process by which man knows reality.* [19]

In this day and age, accepting anything on faith is not only unwise, but also irrational. As has been well articulated by Sam Harris, in no other area of current human endeavor, when the stakes are high, is anything taken on mere faith. We either demand direct proof, strong evidence, or we accept conclusions only from people of proven authority—and that is how it should be. We cannot learn anything trustworthy by means of faith; faith is by definition placing trust in a belief without proof. Of course personal liberties in this country ensure that one may choose to believe on faith whatever one wishes, like the followers of the Heaven's Gate cult who drank cyanide in the belief that they would go to some UFO behind comet Halley-Bopp even though by any measure of logical reasoning this belief is completely misguided [20].

For those who would argue that the Heaven's Gate comparison to Christianity is a stretch, consider this question: Is the belief in some "paradise of the UFO" that much different than the Judeo-Christian belief of how one gets to Heaven? Are the details of how-to and when one goes to heaven really that relevant inasmuch they relate to the concept of faith? Is one alternative to Heaven really much more "realistic" than the other? The answer is: They are not. Faith is faith and only your personal conviction to it makes one alternative (believing it) better than the other (not believing it, or believing something else). Faith does not discriminate between alternative beliefs systems; it cannot discern between a "good" belief and a "bad" belief. That a "bad" belief can become a "good" one is only a matter of the strength of your faith. That is why you really could be a devout Muslim today, a repenting Christian tomorrow, a singing Jew the day after, and a follower of Voodoo in time for the weekend party. In the realm of religious beliefs, who can objectively tell you what belief system is right or wrong? No one.

So we must reach the conclusion that faith is not only a poor substitute for the scientific method, but that in reality it does not offer a way to validate any beliefs we may contemplate regarding the concept of God, even a pantheistic one. We must also come to the full realization that as an organic species living on this planet and for as long as we can formulate a question, a complete understanding of "everything" is simply an unachievable and unrealistic objective. We will remain, for as long as we are around, somewhat ignorant about some aspects of our planet, our solar system, our universe, and ourselves; this is simply the way is it. God is not the answer, God is a cope-out.

4

Jesus as Proof.

Even though I stated earlier that in this discussion we would not focus on any particular religion, I think the figure of Jesus Christ must be addressed. At this point there might be valiant Christian readers who, having made it this far, now ask*: "What about Jesus Christ? Isn't the fact that he did exist proof of the truthfulness of our faith?"* Indeed, the historical figure of Jesus Christ (if he did exist and we can ascertain some facts that connect him to deity) might stand not only as proof of the existence of God, who he claimed was his father, but also as proof that the Christian God is the one "true" God. That is the singular importance of the historical figure of Jesus and why Catholics and other Christians worship him specifically. If it could be demonstrated that Jesus walked this Earth among us, and we can be persuaded he really was the son of God by any means other than faith, we might get closer to having the proof we need for the existence of a universal creator. Ironically, as has already been pointed out, we would not need faith at that stage.

It is interesting to note that, as it happens, Jesus is not the first personage in history to claim the distinction of being the direct offspring of deity; there are other such children. For example, in Greek mythology, Achilles, of Trojan War fame, was the son of the mortal Peleus and the sea nymph goddess Thetis.

The point here is that in the course of human God stories, engendering godlike qualities to offspring has been a common way of providing celestial connections to earthlings. One really ought to examine history to ascertain the veracity of assertions about those other children of deity as proof of other Gods. But putting that aside for the moment, examining Jesus in this manner and removing him from the realm of religious faith (judging the physical evidence as in a "secular" trial), one quickly discovers that Jesus provides little as a matter of evidence for God.

The main question pertaining to Jesus as proof is not really his message. After all, a message of peace, love, and human understanding can be promulgated by anyone (Martin Luther King or Gandhi, for example). The main question is: Does the historical figure of Jesus liberate us from faith? Solving this question to everyone's satisfaction is difficult, as there is little except the Bible to rely on, and the nature of the biblical evidence is both contradictory and self-serving; but we shall give this problem further consideration.

Practically all evidence for the existence of Jesus Christ comes in the form of the four Gospels in the New Testament. It is well known that these four books were written at least 40 years after Jesus' death, at a time when life expectancy was not much more than that. Thus it is fair to assume that none of its authors were actually witnesses to what Jesus said or how he lived. The literacy of most of Jesus' disciples is very much a matter of debate, so whatever testimony survived 40 years must have been preserved primarily by word of mouth.

> . . . the evangelists were only the "spokesmen of the early Christian community which wrote down the oral tradition. For thirty or forty years, the Gospel had existed as an almost exclusively oral tradition: the latter only transmitted sayings and isolated narratives. The evangelists strung them together, each in his own way according to his own character and theological preoccupations. They linked up

the narrations and sayings handed down by the prevailing tradition.
The grouping of Jesus' sayings and likewise the sequence of narratives
is made by the use of fairly vague linking phrases such as 'after this',
'when he had' etc. In other words, the 'framework' of the Synoptic
Gospels is of a purely literary order and is not based on history."
[Cullmann, 1]

How many of us can recite precise conversations that happened say 2 years ago, let alone 40? Also, the natural human propensity to enhance verbal stories brings into question their accuracy. But putting that controversy aside for the moment and assuming Mark, John, Luke and Matthew took appropriate notes of what was going on (although today most scholars believe the Gospels of John, Luke and Matthew are all derived from Mark's), there is the nagging problem that even though all four Gospels are testimonies of the same story, close comparison reveals that many important details do not match. The witnesses in our hypothetical trial do not have their stories straight. Many moderate Christians do not really know the extent and magnitude of the inconsistencies, so I will take the liberty to present some of the more notorious ones.

Take for example, the virgin birth. The singular importance of Jesus' virgin birth is that it matches messianic prophesy in the Old Testament, which was of obvious importance to the Jews, the Gospel's primary audience. In Isaiah 7:14 it is prophesied that:

14 Therefore the Lord himself will give you a sign: The virgin will be
with child and will give birth to a son, and will call him Immanuel
[Immanuel means God with us].

If Jesus was going to be taken seriously as the messiah by his Jewish contemporaries, a virgin birth was a huge point in his favor. There was really no other choice on the matter, otherwise Old Testament prophesy (the word of God) would either have to be ignored or be proven wrong. Ergo, Jesus has a virgin birth, but this crucial point is only mentioned in the Gospels of Luke and Matthew; Mark and John missed this vital issue completely. There is also the well-known fact that Jesus' genealogies do not match from Gospel to Gospel. In Matthew, Jesus lineage is traced back to David's son Salomon, but in Luke it is traced back to David's son Nathan. Besides the fact that the number of generations do not match, they are not even close! In any case, both genealogies get to Jesus through Joseph, which is strange since according to Christian dogma, Joseph was not Jesus' father. Jesus presumably had none of Joseph's DNA. Joseph's lineage is therefore irrelevant since we are told Jesus was the Son of God, so why is it mentioned at all? The genealogy that would be of some relevance was perhaps Mary's, not Joseph's. Mary's genealogy is completely ignored What the Gospels' authors were attempting to do was to link Jesus directly to ancient Jewish royalty in order to enhance his appeal to their mainly Jewish audience. That they also displayed the sexist attitude typical of the male-dominated culture of the times goes without saying.

The Bible, which is put forward as the literal work of the Universal Creator, also appears to be remarkably parochial to Jews and Jewish interests. As an article of faith presumably intended to save all of humankind, this is hard to understand. In particular reference to the New Testament, the fact that Jews were the intended audience of Matthew and Luke is easily realized when one poses the questions: Why would anyone else besides the Jews care who Jesus was related to on his (adoptive) father's side. Why would his lineage be important to the barbaric tribes of what is now Germany or to the Aztec Indians both ultimately forced to convert to Catholicism? As an article of faith, the Aztecs would have cared if Jesus were a proven descendant of Quetzalcoaltl. His relationship to David of the Old Testament would only have meaning to the Jews.

The truth is that in the Bible the inconsistencies are of such magnitude that almost any point of view, and its opposite, is supported at some point. The list of documented inconsistencies below [2] is presented as a small sample, but I believe it proves the point that the Gospels would serve as poor evidence in any objective courtroom:

> *MATTHEW 2:13-16 Following the birth of Jesus, Joseph and Mary flee to Egypt, (where they stay until after Herod's death) in order to avoid the murder of their firstborn by Herod. Herod slaughters all male infants two years old and under. (Note: John the Baptist, Jesus' cousin, though under two is somehow spared without fleeing to Egypt.)*

> *LUKE 2:22-40 Following the birth of Jesus, Joseph and Mary remain in the area of Jerusalem for the Presentation (about forty days) and then return to Nazareth without ever going to Egypt. There is no slaughter of the infants.*

> *MATTHEW 3:11-14, JOHN 1:31-34 John realized the true identity of Jesus (as the Messiah) either prior to the actual Baptism, or from the Baptism onward. The very purpose of John's baptism was to reveal Jesus to Israel.*

> *MATTHEW 11:2-3 After the Baptism, John sends his disciples to ask if Jesus is the Messiah.*

> *MATTHEW 3:16, MARK 1:10 It was Jesus who saw the Spirit descending.*

> *JOHN 1:32 It was John who saw the Spirit descending.*

> *MATTHEW 4:1-11, MARK 1:12-13 Immediately following his Baptism, Jesus spent forty days in the wilderness resisting temptation by the Devil.*

> *JOHN 2:1-11 Three days after the Baptism, Jesus was at the wedding in Cana.*

MATTHEW 4:18-20, MARK 1:16-18 (One story about choosing Peter as a disciple.)

LUKE 5:2-11 (A different story.)

JOHN 1:35-42 (Still another story.)

MATTHEW 5:1-7:29 Jesus delivers his most noteworthy sermon while on the mount.

LUKE 6:17-49 Jesus delivers his most noteworthy sermon while on the plain. (Note: No such sermons are mentioned in either MARK or JOHN and Paul seems totally unfamiliar with the sermon on the mount

MATTHEW 5:22 Anger by itself is a sin.

EP 4:26 Anger is not necessarily a sin.

MATTHEW 5:22 Anger by itself is a sin.

MATTHEW 11:22-24, LUKE 10:13-15 Jesus curses the inhabitants of several cities who are not sufficiently impressed with his mighty works.

MATTHEW 21:19, MARK 11:12-14 Jesus curses a fig tree when it fails to bear fruit out of season.

MATTHEW 5:39, MATTHEW 5:44 Jesus says: "Do not resist evil. Love your enemies."

MATTHEW 6:15, 12:34, 16:3, 22:18, 23:13-15, 17, 19, 27, 29, 33, MARK 7:6, LUKE 11:40, 44, 12:56 Jesus repeatedly hurls epithets at his opponents.

LUKE 19:27 God is likened to one who destroys his enemies.

MATTHEW 5:43-44, MATTHEW 22:39 Love your enemies. Love your neighbor as yourself.

MATTHEW 7:21 Not everyone who calls on the name of the Lord will be saved.

AC 2:21, RO 10:13 Whoever calls on the name of the Lord will be saved.

AC 2:39 Those God calls to himself will be saved.

MATTHEW 7:21, LUKE 10:36-37, RO 2:6, 13, JA 2:24 We are justified by works, not by faith.

JOHN 3:16, RO 3:20-26, EP 2:8-9, GA 2:16 We are justified by faith, not by works.

MATTHEW 10:2, MARK 3:16-19 The twelve apostles (disciples) were: Simon (Peter), Andrew his brother, James the son of Zebedee, John his brother, Philip, Bartholemew, Thomas, Matthew the tax collector, James the son of Alphaeus, Thaddaeus (Labbaeus), Simon, and Judas Iscariot.

LUKE 6:13-16 The above except that Thaddaeus (Labbaeus) is excluded, and Judas the son of James is added (and Judas Iscariot remains).

AC 1:13, 26 Same as MATTHEW and MARK except that, like LUKE Thaddaeus (Labbaeus) is excluded, Judas the son of James is included, and Mathias is chosen by the others to replace Judas Iscariot.

MATTHEW 12:5 Jesus says that the law (Old Testament) states that the priests profane the Sabbath but are blameless. (No such statement is found in the Old Testament).

MATTHEW 12:30 Jesus says that those who are not with him are against him.

MARK 9:40 Jesus says that those who are not against him are for him.

(Note: This puts those who are indifferent or undecided in the "for him" category in the first instance and in the "against him" category in the second instance.)

MATTHEW 13:58, MARK 6:5 In spite of his faith, Jesus is not able to perform mighty miracles.

MATTHEW 17:20, 19:26, MARK 9:23, 10:27, LUKE 17:6, 18:27 Jesus says that anything is possible to him who believes if he has the faith of a grain of mustard seed. All things are possible with God. A mountain can be commanded to move and it will move.

MATTHEW 17:1-2 The Transfiguration occurs six days after Jesus foretells his suffering.

LUKE 9:28-29 It takes place about eight days afterwards.

MATTHEW 23:35 Jesus says that Zacharias (Zechariah) was the son of Barachias (Barachiah).

2CH 24:20 Zacharias was actually the son of Jehoida, the priest. (Note: The name Barachias, or Barachiah, does not appear in the Old Testament)

MATTHEW 24:29-33, MARK 13:24-29 The coming of the kingdom will be accompanied by signs and miracles.

LUKE 17:20-21 It will not be accompanied by signs and miracles. It is already within.

MATTHEW 26:49-50, MARK 14:44-46 Jesus is betrayed by Judas with a kiss, then seized.

LUKE 22:47-48 Jesus anticipates Judas' kiss. No actual kiss is mentioned.

JOHN 18:2-9 Jesus voluntarily steps forward to identify himself making it completely unnecessary for Judas to point him out. No kiss is mentioned.

MATTHEW 26:57, MARK 14:53, LUKE 22:54 After his arrest Jesus is first taken to Caiphas, the high priest.

JOHN 18:13-24 First to Annas, the son-in-law of Caiphas, then to Caiphas.

MATTHEW 26:18-20, 57-68, 27:1-2, MARK 14:16-18, 53-72, 15:1 Jesus' initial hearing was at night on Passover. In the morning he was taken to Pilate.

LUKE 22:13-15, 54-66 The initial hearing took place in the morning on Passover.

JOHN 18:28, 19:14 It took place the day before Passover, on the Day of Preparation.

MATTHEW 26:59-66, MARK 14:55-64 Jesus was tried by the entire Sanhedrin (the chief priests and the whole council).

LUKE 22:66-71 There was no trial but merely an inquiry held by the Sanhedrin.

JOHN 18:13-24 There was no appearance before the Sanhedrin, only the private hearings before Annas and then Caiphas.

MATTHEW 26:63, LUKE 22:70 The high priest asks Jesus if he is the Son of God.

MARK 14:61 He asks Jesus if he is the Son of the Blessed.

MATTHEW 26:64, LUKE 22:70 Jesus answers: "You have said so," or words to this effect.

MARK 14:62 He answers directly: "I am."

MATTHEW 27:5 Judas hanged himself.

AC 1:18 He fell headlong, burst open, and his bowels gushed out.

MATTHEW 27:11, MARK 15:2, LUKE 23:3 When asked if he is King of the Jews, Jesus answers: "You have said so," (or "Thou sayest").

JOHN 18:33-34 He answers: "Do you say this of your own accord?"

MATTHEW 27:11-14 Jesus answers not a single charge at his hearing before Pilate.

JOHN 18:33-37 Jesus answers all charges at his hearing before Pilate.

MATTHEW 27:32, MARK 15:21, LUKE 23:26 Simon of Cyrene carries Jesus' cross.

JOHN 19:17 Jesus carries his own cross with no help from anyone.

MATTHEW 27:46-50, MARK 15:34-37 Jesus' last recorded words are: "My God, my God, why hast thou forsaken me?"

LUKE 23:46 "Father, into thy hands I commit my spirit."

JOHN 19:30 "It is finished." (Note: Even though both MATTHEW and MARK represent direct quotes and are translated similarly, the actual Greek words used for God are different. MATTHEW uses "Eli" and MARK uses "Eloi.")

MATTHEW 27:48, LUKE 23:36, JOHN 19:29 Jesus was offered vinegar to drink.

MARK 15:23 It was wine and myrrh, and he did not drink it.

JOHN 19:29-30 Whatever it was, he did drink it.

MATTHEW 27:62-66 A guard was placed at the tomb (the day following the burial).

MARK 15:42-16:8, LUKE 23:50-56, JOHN 19:38-42 (No guard is mentioned. This is important since rumor had it that Jesus' body was stolen and the Resurrection feigned.)

MARK 16:1-3, LUKE 24:1 (There could not have been a guard, as far as the women were concerned, since they were planning to enter the tomb with spices. Though the women were aware of the stone, they were obviously unaware of a guard.)

MATTHEW 24:9 Even some of the disciples of Jesus will be killed.

JOHN 8:51 If anyone keeps Jesus' words, he will never see death.

HE 9:27 [All] men die once, then judgment follows.

MATTHEW 28:1 The first visitors to the tomb were Mary Magdalene and the other Mary (two).

MARK 16:1 Both of the above plus Salome (three).

LUKE 23:55-24:1, 24:10 Mary Magdalene, Joanna, Mary the mother of James, and "other women" (at least five).

JOHN 20:1 Mary Magdalene only (one).

MATTHEW 28:1 It was toward dawn when they arrived.

MARK 16:2 It was after sunrise.

LUKE 24:1 It was at early dawn.

JOHN 20:1 It was still dark.

MATTHEW 28:1-2 The stone was still in place when they arrived. It was rolled away later.

MARK 16:4, LUKE 24:2, JOHN 20:1 The stone had already been rolled (or taken) away.

MATTHEW 28:2 An angel arrived during an earthquake, rolled back the stone, then sat on it (outside the tomb).

MARK 16:5 No earthquake, only one young man sitting inside the tomb.

LUKE 24:2-4 No earthquake. Two men suddenly appear standing inside the tomb.

JOHN 20:12 No earthquake. Two angels are sitting inside the tomb.

MATTHEW 28:8 The visitors ran to tell the disciples.

MARK 16:8 They said nothing to anyone.

LUKE 24:9 They told the eleven and all the rest.

JOHN 20:10-11 The disciples returned home. Mary remained outside, weeping.

MATTHEW 28:8-9 Jesus' first Resurrection appearance was fairly near the tomb.

LUKE 24:13-15 It was in the vicinity of Emmaus (seven miles from Jerusalem).

JOHN 20:13-14 It was right at the tomb.

MATTHEW 28:9 On his first appearance to them, Jesus lets Mary Magdalene and the other Mary hold him by his feet.

JOHN 20:17 On his first appearance to Mary, Jesus forbids her to touch him since he has not yet ascended to the Father.

JOHN 20:27 A week later, although he has not yet ascended to the Father, Jesus tells Thomas to touch him.

MATTHEW 28:7-10, MATTHEW 28:16 Although some doubted, the initial reaction of those that heard the story was one of belief since they followed the revealed instructions.

MARK 16:11, LUKE 24:11 The initial reaction was one of disbelief. All doubted.

MATTHEW 28:1-18 The order of Resurrection appearances was: Mary Magdalene and the other Mary, then the eleven.

MARK 16:9-14 It was Mary Magdalene, then two others, then the eleven.

LUKE 24:15-36 It was two, then Simon (Peter?), then the eleven.

JOHN 20:14-21:1 It was Mary Magdalene, then the disciples without Thomas, then the disciples with Thomas, then the eleven disciples again.

Corinthians 15:5-8 It was Cephas (Peter?), then the "twelve" (which twelve, Judas was dead?), then 500+ brethren (although Acts 1:15 says there were only about 120), then James, then all the Apostles, then Paul.

MATTHEW 28:19 Jesus instructs his disciples to baptize.

Corinthians 1:17 Although he considers himself a disciple of Jesus, Paul says that he has not been sent to baptize.

MARK 1:2 Jesus quotes a statement that he says appears in Isaiah. (No such statement appears in Isaiah).

MARK 6:16 Herod was the source of the belief that John had been raised from the dead.
LUKE 9:7 Others were the source. Herod was perplexed by the belief.

MARK 6:53 After the feeding of the 5000, Jesus and the disciples went to Gennesaret.

JOHN 6:17-25 They went to Capernaum.

MARK 10:19 Jesus lists "defraud not" as one of the commandments.

EX 20:3-17 There is no such commandment in the Ten Commandments or elsewhere in the Old Testament)

MARK 15:25 It was the third hour when Jesus was crucified.

JOHN 19:14-15 It was after the sixth hour since Jesus was still before Pilate and had not yet been sentenced at that time.

MARK 16:1-2 The women came to the tomb to anoint the body.

JOHN 19:39-40 The body had already been anointed and wrapped in linen cloth.

MARK 16:5, LUKE 24:3 The women actually entered the tomb.

JOHN 20:1-2, 11 They did not.

MARK 16:14-19 The Ascension took place (presumably from a room) while the disciples were together seated at a table, probably in or near Jerusalem.

LUKE 24:50-51 It took place outdoors, after supper, at Bethany (near Jerusalem).

AC 1:9-12 It took place outdoors, after 40+ days, at Mount Olivet.

MATTHEW 28:16-20 No mention is made of an ascension, but if it took place at all, it must have been from a mountain in Galilee since MATTHEW ends there.)

LUKE 14:26 No one can be a disciple of Jesus unless he hates his parents, wife, children, brothers and sisters.

JOHN 3:15 Whoever hates his brother is a murderer.

JOHN 4:20 If anyone claims to love God but hates his brother, he is a liar.

LUKE 23:43 Jesus promises one of those crucified with him that they will be together, that very day, in Paradise.

JOHN 20:17, AC 1:3 Jesus was not raised until the third day and did not ascend until at least forty days later.

LUKE 23:55-56 The women followed Joseph to the tomb, saw how the body had been laid, then went to prepare spices with which to anoint the body.

JOHN 19:39-40 Joseph brought spices with him (75 or a 100 lbs.) and anointed the body (as the women should have noticed).

JOHN 3:17, 8:15, 12:47 Jesus does not judge.

JOHN 5:22, 5:27-30, 9:39, AC 10:42, 2CO 5:10 Jesus does judge.

JOHN 5:22 God does not judge.
RO 2:2-5, 3:19, 2TH 1:5, 1PE 1:17 God does judge.

JOHN 5:24 Believers do not come into judgment.

MATTHEW 12:36, 2CO 5:10, HE 9:27, 1PE 1:17, JU 1:14-15, RE 20:12-13 All persons (including believers) come into judgment.

JOHN 7:38 Jesus quotes a statement that he says appears in scripture (i.e., the Old Testament). (No such statement is found in the Old Testament.)

JOHN 17:12 Mentions a "son of perdition" as appearing in scripture (meaning the Old Testament). (Note: There is no "son of perdition" mentioned in the Old Testament.)

JOHN 20:9 Jesus quotes a statement that he says appears in scripture (meaning the Old Testament). (No such statement is found in the Old Testament.)

Acts 19-28 Shortly after his conversion, Paul went to Damascus, then Jerusalem where he was introduced to the Apostles by Barnabas, and there spent some time with them (going in and out among them).

Galatians 1:15-20 He made the trip three years later, then saw only Peter and James.

Acts 20:35 Quotes Jesus as having said: "It is more blessed to give than to receive." (No such statement by Jesus is found elsewhere in the Bible.)

The inconsistencies above are by no means the only ones. But after examining just the evidence above, any objective observer would have to conclude that as the presumed literal work of the universal creator, the Gospels are a very poor accomplishment. The many inconsistencies lend strong support to the notion that these writings are all based on oral tradition carried on by early Christian preachers, and that there is one primary source (presumably Mark's) which was copied and recopied several times with different degrees of success, and with multiple and liberal additions.

Despite the fact that these inconsistencies (and others) are well known, many theist scholars have come up with rationalizations, albeit unconvincing ones, for each of them. Moreover, our valiant Christian friends might argue that we are quibbling over minor details.

Therefore, let us for argument's sake ignore all which brings doubt to the veracity of the Biblical New Testament. Let us forget all other children of gods in the whole of human religious experience. Let us pay no attention to the fact that the Bible appears to be a book specifically written by and for the Jewish people (not God's testament for all humankind). Let us put aside the fact that the story of Jesus in the New Testament was authored by people who did not know him personally, and thus the story of Jesus is based on hearsay. Let's ignore the plethora of Biblical inconsistencies, which of course suggests the story is a work of fiction. Ignoring all of this (which is quite a lot), and taking for granted therefore that he walked among us humans, ultimately when it comes to the figure of Jesus as proof of God's existence there are two possibilities: he either was the son of God as he claimed, or he was delusional or lying. So we need to ascertain the historical Jesus as the possible only begotten son of the Universal Creator based on his acts, the mission he was given, and the results thereafter, taking the Bible as irrefutable testimony.

Thus, according to the Bible, the universal creator sent Jesus to the Israelites, as opposed to say the Romans, the Aztecs, or the Mongolians, because the creator had a previous covenant with the Jews that made them particularly special in His eyes. Jesus seemed to have had at least four major objectives to accomplish while on this planet. First, to convince the majority of the Jews that he was indeed the messiah as prophesied in the Old Testament; second, to urge the Jews to repent their sins because Judgment Day was imminent; third, (and here it gets dicey) to form a new church; and fourth; to die suffering to atone the sins of humanity.

> . . . *much of the teaching of the gospel was uttered in view of an impending catastrophe and liquidation of this world's affairs, out of which, at a wave of the divine wand, a new and blessed condition was to emerge, just as the phoenix arises, renewed and immortal, out of its own ashes. Jesus felt himself to be the harbinger of a new and divine constitution . . . . To be suddenly imposed by divine power and interference. Hence the precepts to follow him; to forsake parents, wife, children and home; even to neglect the most sacred of all ancient duties—that of burying one's own father* [Frederick Conybeare, 3].

Jesus said to him, "Let the dead bury their own dead, but you go and proclaim the kingdom of God." [Luke 9:59-61].

From that time on Jesus began to preach, "Repent, for the kingdom of heaven is near." [Matthew 4:17]

Incidentally, at least in one instance, it seems that Jesus did not come to save the whole of humanity from the impending debacle—far from it. Jews, or converted Jews, were the primary and exclusive targets.

When he was alone, the Twelve and the others around him asked him about the parables. He told them, "The secret of the kingdom of God has been given to you. But to those on the outside everything is said in parables so that, they may be ever seeing but never perceiving, and ever hearing but never understanding; otherwise they might turn and be forgiven!" [Mark 4:10-12]

This passage is quite astounding as it suggests Jesus really did not want everyone to be forgiven. The "love thy neighbor" moral and philosophical teaching of forgiveness appears to be secondary to the main objectives of his visit. As it happens often in the Bible, other passages seem to suggest the complete opposite. In any case, the message of the imminent second coming has endured to this day and is one of the main reasons Christians strongly urge everyone to promptly join them in accepting their beliefs. Of course, we all know what happens if we are not convinced.

Regardless, in order to be taken seriously on his warning of Judgment Day, Jesus had to convince the Jews of his deity (his first objective), and in this regard he failed miserably. The vast majority of Jews of his time did not believe him to be the prophesied messiah. Not the priests, not the general populace, only a handful of people. In fact, Jews today are still waiting for their messiah.

[The Claims of Jesus About Himself] The Jews answered him, "Aren't we right in saying that you are a Samaritan and demon-possessed?" [John 8:47-49].

[The Jews Continue in Their Unbelief] Even after Jesus had done all these miraculous signs in their presence, they still would not believe in him. [John 12:36-38].

Then Jesus declared, "I am the bread of life. He who comes to me will never go hungry, and he who believes in me will never be thirsty. But as I told you, you have seen me and still you do not believe. [John 6:35-36]

At this the Jews began to grumble about him because he said, "I am the bread that came down from heaven." They said, "Is this not Jesus, the son of Joseph, whose father and mother we know? How can he now say, 'I came down from heaven'?"

"Stop grumbling among yourselves," Jesus answered. "No one can come to me unless the Father who sent me draws him, and I will raise him up at the last day. [John 6:41-44]

This last passage from John suggests that the Jews had to take him as the Son of God on faith. Not even his death on the cross was enough to convince the Jews. It is interesting to note that in the end, the only thing Jesus had to do to convince large numbers of people regarding the true nature of his deity was to go public after his crucifixion and rise from the dead. Had he shown himself back in Herod's palace, or to the Jewish priests who had a hand in sending him to the cross, or had he ascended to the Heavens in front of the general public in Jerusalem's main square, not only would the news appear prominently in the Roman archives (which are essentially silent on the historical figure of Jesus), but the Jewish community would have been seriously impressed. It would have been a marketing *coup de main*. An easily corroborated and multi-sourced account of his ascension to heaven would serve nicely as proof of his god-like powers. This of course did not happen and we are left with mystery, innuendo, hearsay, and contradiction.

Moving on, the impending cosmic disaster that Jesus came to warn us about, (his second objective) did not materialize. Indeed, Christians have been anxiously waiting for it ever since:

And he said to them, "I tell you the truth, some who are standing here will not taste death before they see the kingdom of God come with power." [Mark 9:1].

Not only did all those who presumably heard Jesus' warning above "taste death", but so have about 80 generations after them in the span of two millennia. So Jesus not only did not achieve the mission he was sent here for as far as the Jews are concerned; but the very thing he came to warn us about (i.e. Judgment Day) did not and has not materialized. Now, biblical apologetics have argued that the time and date was not stipulated exactly, and Matthew and Peter later in the Bible reject any attempts to be pinned down to specifics. But to those who presumably heard the above passage from Jesus as recorded by Mark, the message was pretty clear. Fussiness on this issue has come from others; obviously the presumption that He is indeed coming at all is an article of faith. To the extent that Jesus suggested the second coming was imminent, and his call to put everything aside and proclaim the coming of the Kingdom of God does suggest such a thing, he has been proven wrong.

His third mission, to create a new Church, is somewhat fuzzy, but again this is not atypical of the Bible.

Jesus replied, "Blessed are you, Simon son of Jonah, for this was not revealed to you by man, but by my Father in heaven. And I tell you that you are Peter and on this rock I will build my church, and the gates of Hades will not overcome it. I will give you the keys of the kingdom of heaven; whatever you bind on earth will be found in heaven, and whatever you loose on earth will be loosed in heaven." [Matthew 16:17-19].

In recounting this same episode Marks fail to mention anything about a church [see Mark 8:27-30]. There is no evidence that Jesus regarded himself as being anything other than a Jew, so it is strange that he wanted to launch the formation of a completely new alternative religion based on worshiping him personally. Of course, there is a self-serving element to this celestial mandate. The Catholic Encyclopedia explains:

> *By the word "rock" the Saviour cannot have meant Himself, but only Peter, as is so much more apparent in Aramaic in which the same word (Kipha) is used for "Peter" and "rock". His statement then admits of but one explanation, namely, that He wishes to make Peter the head of the whole community of those who believed in Him as the true Messiah; that through this foundation (Peter) the Kingdom of Christ would be unconquerable; that the spiritual guidance of the faithful was placed in the hands of Peter, as the special representative of Christ. This meaning becomes so much clearer when we remember that the words "bind" and "loose" are not metaphorical, but Jewish juridical terms. It is also clear that the position of Peter among the other Apostles and in the Christian community was the basis for the Kingdom of God on earth, that is, the Church of Christ. Peter was personally installed as Head of the Apostles by Christ Himself. This foundation created for the Church by its Founder could not disappear with the person of Peter, but was intended to continue and did continue (as actual history shows) in the primacy of the Roman Church and its bishops. Entirely inconsistent and in itself untenable is the position of Protestants who (like Schnitzer in recent times) assert that the primacy of the Roman bishops cannot be deduced from the precedence which Peter held among the Apostles.* [4]

In any case, one end result of the fuzziness in these instructions has been, as the historic record shows, centuries of war between Christian factions and against other established churches, causing hundreds of thousands of human casualties. So assuming the "successful" foundation of a church based on the worship of Jesus Christ as proof of God existence is a tenuous proposition at best.

We must realize that the whole Christian apostolate as presently constituted was not Jesus' personal achievement; he was already dead and presumably in Heaven. The creation of the many churches that we know today was very much the work of other *bona fide* humans, work that stands, in my view, as one of the most colossal public relations, marketing, psychological, and political achievements in the history of humanity. The argument could be made that at least some of success in the spread of Christianity can be attributed to Jesus' message of love thy neighbor as you love yourself; and that all Jesus had to do was to implant the seed. However, there is really nothing celestial about the idea that we must get along with one another; Jews, gentiles, Muslims and Christians. Yes, the message is indeed powerful in that it makes perfect sense; but a testament of God's existence is not. We should indeed get along together if we want to survive, prosper and be happy; the idea is entirely humanistic in nature and not even unique to Jesus. Other both ancient and modern philosophical traditions carry the same message.

His fourth mission was presumably to be painfully killed in order to atone for the sins of humanity. The Catholic Encyclopedia explains:

> *That man should be delivered by Christ's Passion was in keeping with both His mercy and His justice. With His justice, because by His Passion Christ made satisfaction for the sin of the human race; and so man was set free by Christ's justice: and with His mercy, for since man of himself could not satisfy for the sin of all human nature, God gave him His Son to satisfy for him,* [5]
>
> *From the beginning of His conception Christ merited our eternal salvation; but on our side there were some obstacles, whereby we were hindered from securing the effect of His preceding merits: consequently, in order to remove such hindrances, "it was necessary for Christ to suffer."* [6]

This is presumably his most important mission of all: to save us from hell by being brutally murdered. He had to be murdered; he could not simply die. Jesus had to suffer as a matter of principle. He had to suffer presumably by heavenly mandate. And only He could save us, because *man himself could not satisfy for the sin of all human nature.* God required *satisfaction.* As we have seen, the reasons for Jesus' suffering are not really to serve as "shock and awe" example to everyone of the brutality humankind is capable of (humans in the first century had already plenty of those), but *in order to remove hindrances.* That is, the universal creator demanded blood, and He demanded suffering. God was not willing to forgive our sins, not even those of the yet unborn, without the heavy penalty of a blood sacrifice. And sacrifice by man himself was not enough to appease Him.

The reasons why the universal creator would demand blood sacrifice cannot be either explained convincingly, or understood by logical reasoning. This would presume that in our universe there appears to exist a form of cosmic tax collector, who trades sin redemption with suffering credits, which has to be appeased. This individual, who presumably is God Himself, was not willing to waive the suffering tax, so he tortured his own son to pay for it. Actually, his son was the only one with a big enough credit line to pay for all humanity, as we are told man himself could not provide enough *satisfaction.* In my opinion, this line of reasoning is ridiculous at so many levels that I will not spend much time discussing it. In any case, that these are indeed the reasons behind Jesus' crucifixion is a matter of dogma and an article of faith; thus it cannot serve as proof of God's existence. Quite the contrary.

So, putting all these things together we have that the very existence of Jesus is open to question given the unreliable sources, excessive contradictions, and inconsistent nature of the Biblical scriptures. Even if he did exist, his message proved to be not only inconsequential (he did not convert many people in *his* time) but also incorrect, as the second coming has proven not to be the imminent catastrophe he led his contemporaries to believe. In fact, his believers are still waiting **two millennia** later. The creation of a church in his name has only caused direct conflict among humans, and considering the tortuous history of atrocities committed by all his churches combined, it can hardly be considered either proof of a loving God or a success as far as a step forward for humanity. That Jesus had to die suffering really proves nothing, except that if one believes this religious mythology, we accept that we are dealing with a blood thirsty God who trades in human pain and anguish.

Ultimately, there are simply too many questions unanswered, too many important issues left unclear, and too many inconsistencies. The Bible is rife with definitive statements that are later contradicted. It is impossible to reach a definitive conclusion about almost any substantive questions, even moral ones, by reading the Bible. By himself, without the aid of all other influential personalities and political imposition that came after him, Jesus' life stands as a very modest singular achievement by the universal creator, if He indeed wanted Jesus to mediate salvation for us. Jesus does not liberate us from having to rely on faith to get to God. He does not validate God's existence; ultimately he represents poor evidence for the existence of the very God he said he was here on behalf of.

Personally, I find baffling the underlying logic of the Christian God. We are supposed to accept the existence of a supreme being of unfathomable superpowers who demands our worship under penalty of everlasting suffering in the afterlife. And we are to accept this on nothing but the flimsiest of evidence. Evidence, I should add, that is over two thousand years old, rife with contradictions, and does not make any logical sense. Why would such a being demand personal worship from the likes of us? Compared with the magnificence of the whole universe, we are nothing, tantamount to bacteria growing on a rock, and probably not even unique. Why the perverse infatuation with human suffering? We have seen that by design Christ had to suffer to atone our sins, and we humans are supposed to endure a life through a "valley of tears". Hell, the inescapable destiny for most of humankind, is *designed* to impart the greatest amount of pain on unbelievers *for eternity*. Why the purposeful celestial silence for so long? Why hasn't God come out and unequivocally told everyone clearly what He wants? What is the purpose of confusing humans with competing spiritual beliefs and relying on wacky religious leaders? Why play games with the human species? It makes no sense., that is why faith is needed.

5

What About Pascal?

M any people, knowingly or not, have assumed the posture first articulated by Blaise Pascal (1623-1662) that proposes one should believe in God because given the massive potential rewards in favor, and dire consequences against, believing in the existence of God is a better bet than otherwise:

> *Blaise Pascal offers a pragmatic reason for believing in God: even under the assumption that God's existence is unlikely, the potential benefits of believing are so vast as to make betting on theism rational.* [Highlights added, 1]

If one is contemplating a reason to believe in God, Pascal's wager, as this line of reasoning is called, may seem like a good one, and today many moderate Christians in America prescribe to its basic logic.

The rationale goes like this: Believe in God because there is no real downside; nothing is particularly troublesome or bad about not believing. What in essence is one putting on the table to wage against believing? If one is Catholic, for example, it does not seem to be asking too much to believe in a good God, behave decently toward others, obey certain reasonable laws, and go to church every Sunday. If one chooses to ignore some of the more burdensome dogmatic mandates (like using contraceptives or having sex before marriage, or for reasons other than procreation), it is probably okay since we are dealing with a presumed benevolent God anyway. One may feel that by following at least some of the more important mandates (which include having faith, of course), Heaven may be a very real possibility; and if there is no God or Heaven, one is no worse off for believing there is. By going to church we interact with others in the community, talk about important issues, and either help advance noble causes or embark on some ourselves—is all good. This is the "easy chair" theism of the moderates, as opposed to the fundamentalist-militant form of theism espoused by Osama bin Laden and Jerry Falwell.

If one is not really serious about the question of whether or not God exists, or one does not care about stances a particular church supports, then "easy-chair" theism is fine. Take the wager and use Pascal's logic as the basis for your belief. Accepting Pascal's wager implies that one is prepared to lose; it is just that the payoff is so huge and investment so modest that it makes a very reasonable bet. It's like investing $5 in tickets for the $300,000,000 super jackpot lotto even though you know your chances of winning are negligible. In this lottery example, just like in Pascal's wager, you do not care if you lose. After all, you only put in $5, and you like talking to the guy at the ticket counter anyway. You would like to win, of course, but if you do not, your losses have been minimal.

If one is not determined to implement "the will of God" by political and/or military action, then this "easy-chair" theism is also fine, so take the wager. Since accepting Pascal's wager implies you are assessing probabilities, then you have in essence accepted at least some *possibility* that there is no God. Therefore the concept of God is at least questionable—a question you have elected to put aside for the moment, until the bet is settled. But if the existence of God is questionable to some degree, what about his presumed will? Where does the "will of God" come from? If there is no God, there obviously cannot be a "will of God". If the probability that God exists is one in twenty million, then the will of God is right up there with mandates from the Psychic Hotline. But if there is a chance, even a small one, that the "word of God" is fiction, is it fair to impose it on others?

If, on the other hand, you are serious about implementing the presumed will of your God by political action, if you are serious enough to allow your children to blow themselves up for your God, or to make homosexuality and abortion illegal, or impose the Christian Ten Commandments in a secular courthouse, or make specific scientific research illegal, or to curtail the teaching of biology in public schools, or to support such actions by your vote, then you must care enough to go through the trouble of finding out what is the case for God's existence. The more serious you are about implementing the "will of God", the more serious you have to be about answering the question of whether or not God truly exists. Pascal's wager is really the lazy way out of this problem, and as such has been called immoral and irresponsible. What you have placed on the table to wage against is your capacity to take a serious moral stance on issues using your belief in God as a basis; you are in a "wait-and-see" mode, you are playing the odds.

Of course some people want it both ways; they use the loosy-goosy "easy-chair" theism of Pascal's wager, and they feel morally warranted, self-righteous, and completely justified about voting to "protect marriage" or to "cultivate a culture of life". It is not all good, what if you lose your bet? In that case you have imposed some arbitrary, unfair, baseless, and ridiculous restrictions on countless people's lives because of your inability to correctly gauge probabilities. If one is betting, one cannot take any action until the bet is settled. Since settling this particular bet requires that you die, Pascal's wager is crazy.

> *Critics in turn have raised a number of now-classic challenges* [to Pascal's wager]. *According to Intellectualism, deliberately choosing which beliefs to hold is practically impossible; according to the Many-gods Objection, Pascal's wager begs the question and hence is irrational; according to Evidentialism, Pascalian reasoning is epistemically irresponsible and hence immoral; and according to various paradoxes, reference to infinite values is decision-theoretic nonsense.* [1]

Osama bin Laden and others like him have not taken Pascal's wager. In their view there are no probabilistic ambiguities, they are totally sure of the outcome and are putting their lives on the line to support and defend their beliefs. They have bought the mansion and the yacht on credit before the official announcement of who has the winning lottery ticket.

There is a body of work critical of Pascal's reasoning for believing in the existence of God. Since Pascal was a mathematician, most of his arguments were made in the language of formal logic, and thus critiques of his ideas are also in this language. For anyone interested in plunging into this interesting philosophical discourse, a list of suggestions is presented in reference 2, see also Sam Harris' commentary on Pascal in reference 3.

George Smith has offered a counter wager that I personally like much better [4]. It goes like this: If there is a God, we can start by assuming He is either a moral God, or an evil God. Given that He has given us no evidence to support His existence commensurate with His tremendous accomplishments in the creation of the universe; given that He has offered no conclusive communiqué of His wishes or desires, no unequivocal mission or objectives; given that He has left us completely alone, then, if He is a moral God, He cannot fault us for questioning His very existence. He cannot fault us for correctly utilizing the faculty of logical reasoning He Himself gave us. Thus, forgiveness for the sin of non-belief is a good bet if we are dealing with a moral God.

If, on the other hand, God is evil, then whether one believes in His existence or not is irrelevant to our prospects in the afterlife. An evil God may wish to treat us in completely irrational, mean, arbitrary, and unfair ways, regardless of our beliefs and our actions on this planet.

Therefore, use your logical judgment and do not entertain irrational beliefs about afterlife because either way it will be inconsequential: God will either not care and forgive you, or will torture you for eternity no matter what you believe.

6

Religion and Morality.

A s presented previously, one aspect that religious dogma—defined for this discussion as the doctrinal application at ground level of the concept of God—has greatly simplified for the human masses is deciding what can be considered moral behavior and what cannot. This is so because by one definition, moral behavior is that which is sanctioned by God, or derived from His teachings. This is the conundrum where we began our journey. A particular God and associated dogma as a starting principle for moral behavior is a common theme in all religions, but nowhere is there a better example than in the biblical story of Moses coming down from Mount Sinai with the Ten Commandments. This story settles the issue unequivocally for Jews and Christians; God laid down the law.

The problem with a moral code not based on some religious doctrine is that it becomes debatable, or at least more debatable than otherwise. No one can debate the presumed "word of God", but we all can debate the word of our fellow humans. For example, if there is no God to forbid it, why is homosexuality "bad"? Why is abortion "bad"? What is the basis for this judgment? How are we going to decide these complicated questions? If we abandon a law-giving, justice-dispensing, judge-God, by what process, hopefully rational, do we reach consensus on what is "good" and what is "bad" both in word and deed? The attack by the Christian right on "secularism" is based in large part on the fact that they see all debate on homosexuality, abortion, and other such issues as irrelevant, because the question has already been settled by God himself!

> *The Bible is very clear—homosexuality is an abomination, and I do think homosexual marriage should be illegal. This is just not my opinion. This is God's opinion.* [Mary Ann Markarian, 1]

Take killing people, for example. Killing for money is bad, but killing in war (with professional soldiers) is okay; it is even demanded sometimes. Killing humans within the context of a government sponsored justice system (known as capital punishment in the United States and other countries) is also sanctioned. Killing is even okay if done in the name of God. In fact, a man in US-liberated Afghanistan almost went on trial under penalty of death for converting from Islam to Christianity [2].

> *. . . a statement like "Murder is wrong" while being uncontroversial in most circles, has never seemed anchored to the facts of this world in the way that statements about planets or molecules appear to be. The problem, in philosophical terms, has been one of characterizing just what sort of "facts" our moral intuitions can be said to track—if indeed they track anything of the kind.* [Sam Harris, 3]

Sam Harris has proposed that there might be a physiological connection to what we perceive as "good" and "bad" behavior. That somehow "good" and "bad" feel like they do because of some fundamental brain wiring. Although this is an interesting proposal, it may take many years of research to judge this idea conclusively. In any case, I suspect that few Christians will be persuaded to move away from millennia of God-defined morality by an alternative interpretation of neural connections and/or enzymatic biochemistry.

However, that a moral code of behavior may be debatable does not mean that a good one cannot be formulated. In my opinion, philosophers have over-analyzed and over-complicated this question of debatable morality, at least in how a secular moral code, as opposed to a religiously derived one, has to be derived or justified to be used at a personal or even at the government level. The fact is that God, if He indeed exists, has probably had little to do with our laws, and yet we have a working judicial system already—perhaps derived under false pretenses and far from perfect, but a working system nevertheless. At the very least it is a system that could stand as a solid starting point, without having to create one from scratch.

For example, an ethical system that ensures *Life, Liberty and the pursuit of Happiness* for each individual without depriving others of the same sounds acceptable and fair. I agree with Harris' statement that:

> *To treat others ethically is to act out of concern for their happiness and suffering.*

Sam Harris continues:

> *There is a circle here that links us to one another: we each want to be happy; the social feeling of love is one of our greatest sources of happiness; and love entails that we be concerned for the happiness of others. We discover that we can be selfish together.* [4]

Here is another relevant quote from a second serious atheist:

> *If man is to survive, he must have knowledge of those principles of action conducive to survival. And, beyond the level of mere survival, if man is to achieve happiness he must have knowledge of those principles of action conducive to happiness. Man must discover, through a process of reason, the values required for his survival and well being.* [George H. Smith, 5]

From my perspective there is really not a large gap between accepting the rights of everyone for *Life Liberty and the pursuit of Happiness* and accepting that:

13. Thou shalt not kill.

14. Thou shalt not commit adultery.

15. Thou shalt not steal.

16. Thou shalt not bear false witness against thy neighbor.

17. Thou shalt not covet thy neighbor's house, thou shalt not covet thy neighbor's wife, nor his manservant, nor his maidservant, nor his ox, nor his ass, nor any thing that is thy neighbor's. [Exodus 20:13-17].

One could see the rules above as part of a simple instruction manual for societal cohabitation. I would argue that the above excerpt from Exodus is at least partly a moral code to ensure *Life, Liberty and the pursuit of Happiness* presented in the necessary mystical and superstitious veil that the Israelites required for acceptance thousands of years ago. In fact, a mystical, superstitious, and cosmically threatening veil was probably the only way of ensuring the majority of people ware going to follow these moral codes 3000 years ago, and maybe even some people today. Philosophical rationalities were not going to do it.

I am not suggesting even for a second that the authors of the Old Testament launched the greatest religious hoax of the last three thousand years. The authors of the Old Testament believed deeply in their God, and their followers believed their writings came directly from the Universal Creator himself, as many believers still do to this day. What I am saying is that, ironically, if we take out God and all associated incongruities and nonsense (which actually covers a lot), as far as a personal moral code of behavior and a basis for an ethical system of secular laws is concerned, this secular model is a perfectly acceptable one. All we need to do is take out the idea that some God *told* us these things. We need to dispense with the notion that the moral underpinnings, inasmuch as they relate to how we ought to behave towards each other, came from the heavens. However, they do represent a step forward in preserving the peace of the tribe and maximizing the chances of *Life, Liberty and the pursuit of Happiness.*

What I am saying is this: I am in agreement with those that endorse the idea that to behave morally is to act towards others out of concern for their feelings, their health, their suffering, and their happiness. The basis for a rationally derived moral code of behavior should start from the proposition that humans need to treat each other with an appreciation for the fulfillment of each individual life's ambitions and dreams, their personal liberty to act and feel as they would like as long as it does not infringe on others, and to pursue their individual happiness, again as long as it does not infringe on that of others. I cannot envision this causing much debate. If one really is in need of a list, I would argue that a review of human history and psyche suggests several very simple rules that at the personal level help promote and ensure this objective. There is no need to rely on complicated philosophical reasonings. I state them in the simplest of terms as:

1. *To behave morally is to act out of concern for the feelings, wellbeing, and the suffering of others.*
2. *Work for your own happiness andf that of your loved ones, without infringing on the right of others to do the same. This means at least:*

    a. *Don't take other people's life away.*
    b. *Don't take property that is not yours.*
    c. *Don't lie to others (particularly your spouse), always be honest with yourself and others.*

2. *Keep all other laws designed to maintain the peace of the tribe.*

I freely admit this is a simplistic presentation, but my main point is that a concept of God is not essential to formulate a true, workable and robust moral code of behavior. In fact, a moral code of behavior based on the simple idea that we all have the right to enjoy this life leads to many of the same important rules that people think come from believing in a universal creator. This is so because one of the objectives of moral codes of behavior derived from our beliefs in gods was to ensure the peace of the tribe. Our American system of government, where there is supposed to be strict separation of church and state, is a good example of how a "secular" form of government can be instituted. I find insulting the idea that humans will descend into anarchy, chaos, and murder without some threat of cosmic or divine revenge.

> *Secularism: Secularism is a code of duty pertaining to this life, founded on considerations purely human, and intended mainly for those who find theology indefinite or inadequate, unreliable or unbelievable. Its essential principles are three:*
>
> *(1) The improvement of this life by material means.*
> *(2) That science is the available Providence of man.*
> *(3) That it is good to do good. Whether there be other good or not, the good of the present life is good, and it is good to seek that good.*

[*Holyoake's 1896 publication English Secularism, 6*]

Serious problems will ensue, however, with the inclusion of the concept of God in a pluralistic liberal society like ours because it introduces other bases for presumed moral behavior that are irrational and contrary to fostering the peace of the tribe, especially a big, heterogeneous "tribe" like the one we have in the United States. Once you introduce the concept of God, you must hypothesize his presumed wishes, desires, and other preoccupations that are not only based on fantasy, but also have been proven to be detrimental to the peace of the tribe. These arguments are almost as old as the Republic.

> *We must trace a line of distinction between those that are capable of verification, and those that are not, and separate by an inviolable barrier the world of fantastical beings from the world of realities; that is to say, all civil effect must be taken away from theological and religious opinions.* [C. F. Volney, 7]

What is important to realize is that democratic governments lay a foundation to protect and ensure the happiness of their citizens as defined by them. Laws are needed to ensure one person's right not to infringe on the rights of others, but laws should not be created to appease some God of the Volcano or the God of Heaven. We must be vigilant to attacks on secularism on the premise of following some hypothetical "higher power". In terms of what constitutes and what does not constitute moral behavior we must first ask ourselves if the action infringes on anyone else's ability to pursue his or her happiness, or if some third person's civil or human rights are being infringed or violated. Even if we personally consider the behavior reprehensible or in some form ugly or disagreeable, we really have no right to impose any of our cosmically derived ideas of morality upon anyone.

In America at present some have taken a distorted view or presumed "moral values" to new levels. At this stage in our collective history it is shocking that some people want to drag the rest of us back to the time of the Inquisition. There is simply no excuse to curtail stem cell research on the basis of "fostering a culture of life". Curtailment of stem cell research is not acting out of concern for people's suffering and happiness, totally to the contrary. Religious fanatics purposely put aside the fact that this research is being conducted precisely to enhance the quality of life for many and latch on to some misguided idea of moral behavior.

So, in conclusion, it is possible to derive a moral code of behavior independent from the concept of God. In fact, in attempting to come up with one with the objective of ensuring *Life, Liberty and the Pursuit of Happiness* we discover that many of the basic moral tenets of Judeo-Christian religions come up naturally. We can indeed develop laws to ensure the peace of the tribe without resorting to ideas of celestial mandates. In fact, when considering a pluralistic society, like one made largely of immigrants, for example, keeping God out of the process of making laws is a very good idea. The historic record indicates that this is precisely what the Founding Fathers wanted to accomplish in this country so that its citizens could worship within any religion they wished, or none at all.

7

A Beautiful Life.

From my standpoint there is a level of maturity that comes from ultimately realizing the fallacy of the concept of God. It is not much different than the human rite of passage of leaving home and finally taking charge of one's life away from one's parents. As in the leaving-home example there is an element of sadness, nostalgia, and heartbreak involved in the process. A similar set of feelings ensues when we discover that Santa Claus does not exist. Even though most of us were young children at the time, most people can remember when they finally found out the truth about Santa, and in most cases there was a sense of loss, sad surprise, and some form of disappointment. There is beautiful magic and wholesome goodness in a world where Santa is alive, real, and actively doing all the things Santa does. Just as there is beautiful magic and hope in a world of angels and Heaven and where a benevolent and infinitively wise God intervenes on our behalf. Is it that much of a stretch to consider that the concept of God is nothing more than Santa for grownups? Are the two concepts really that different? Are the adults of our species that much more attuned to reality than our children not to deceive themselves with this type of superstition?

There is no denying that for vast numbers of people life is not full of happiness. We are all witnesses to real injustices and human cruelty on the scale of many thousands. In addition there are also personal, physical, and psychological struggles of every kind that many of us have to endure. In the face of a lifetime of toil, disappointment, stress, pain, personal loss, and ultimate death what is there to supply the energy to carry on? Why carry on at all? What's the point? Is the idea of an afterlife in a peaceful place of absolute bliss, where we can again meet our long-departed love ones, appealing? Is the idea of that prospect, even if it is only a very remote one, appealing and comforting enough that we are willing to ignore all the impossibilities that encompass this prospect and still believe in it? I think the answer for many people is yes. I am convinced large numbers of people are willing to forego rational thought on this issue on the mere hope that such a place does exist. More than that even, large numbers of humans are willing to deprive themselves of marriage and sex, of speaking or eating for periods of time, or are willing to inflict pain on themselves or others if they believe it will help them "earn" their way into an everlasting afterlife.

When times are hard, people move to God and to spirituality. In the current times of uncertainty and world terrorism a sense of panic appears to have consumed our country. Some theologians argue that Americans appear to have moved to the Right politically presumably in search of moral values and spirituality, or at least because the Right is not embarrassed to talk about spirituality. In these bad times the Left's failure to address our natural need for spirituality, or for having some concept of life's meaning, has thus resulted in Americans migrating to the Christian Right. In studying this trend Michael Lerner [1] has concluded that people need . . .

> . . . a spiritual framework that can lend meaning to [their] lives. [People] yearn for a purpose-driven life that will allow them to serve something beyond personal goals and economic self-interest. If they don't find this sense of purpose on the Left, they will look for it on the Right.

He continues,

People earning close to the median income in the United States told us that they wondered what their life was really about, what the purpose of living was, what they could tell their children they had achieved while living on this planet.

Many people talked about the missing element in terms of a cheapening of work itself—that once it had been separated from the idea of a higher mission or purpose, work became vulgar or debased.

People repeatedly mentioned that work made them feel deadened inside . . . This spiritual depression is characterized by a sense of loneliness or alienation, a feeling that we are not really being recognized or dealt with in an authentic way . . . a loss of awareness of the beauty and holiness that surrounds us.

Americans are thus presumably drawn to the Right because only the Right is addressing this spiritual vacuum, whereas the Left is silent on this theme. The voting public is thus interpreting this silence as, at best, the Left having no position on the subject or, at worst, being repulsed by it.

I think it cannot be denied that humans at some level require some form of "spirituality," although it is rather difficult to pinpoint what spirituality means exactly or what the precise form of this need actually is. This need seems to be as diverse as humans themselves.

Spirituality: The state, quality, manner, or fact of being spiritual. [2]

Spiritual: Of, relating to, consisting of, or having the nature of spirit; not tangible or material. [2]

Spirituality is, in a narrow sense, a concern with matters of the spirit. The spiritual, concerning as it does with eternal verities regarding Man's ultimate nature, is often contrasted with the temporal or the worldly. The central defining characteristic of spirituality is a sense of connection to a much greater whole which includes an emotional experience of religious awe and reverence. As with some forms of religion, the emphasis of spirituality is often on personal experience. It may be an expression for life perceived as higher, more complex or more integrated with one's worldview, as contrasted with the merely sensual. [3]

Often people can feel a connection to some *much greater whole* (thus a sense of spirituality) by simply admiring a sunset, or going for a quiet sail on the ocean or a lake. In this way some feel they are witnesses of Creation, and thus connected to the universe (or God) by being conscious spectators of the magnificence of Nature. Many astronauts have come back from space with a greater connection with the world after observing first hand our fragile planet as one whole entity with no visible frontiers. Others seem to require much more, such as a strong belief in supernatural beings and their presumed interventions, plus a full and complex spiritual world parallel to ours.

But why do humans, Lerner's unhappy overworked Americans in particular, have a specific psychological *need* to "believe in something" bigger than themselves or the world around them? Can this need be partly a reflection of psychological stress and uncertainty? Can this be explained, at least partially, as an underlying lack of perspective regarding the human experience, or having to endure an unfulfilled and/or unhappy personal or work life? Does "spirituality" actually explain and thus fulfill one's life, or can one fulfill one's life with "spirituality"? (paraphrasing Richard Dawkings; filling a much needed gap?) Can this need for "spirituality" be the result of a need to exercise our imagination, or is "spirituality" simply an offshoot of the human sense of self, part of the feeling of awe regarding our own existence?

In any case, how does the belief in an intangible and inaccessible (in life) spirit world actually bring a *"connection to a much greater whole"*; are we not in effect disconnected, or "connected" only by Faith? Besides, inasmuch as "spirituality" attempts to explain something about life's meaning, if we can question the meaning of *this* life, why can't we question the meaning of the next one?

This need for "spirituality" touches on issues related to psychology, sociology, philosophy, economics, and culture, among many. As such it is probably impossible to address it as a single topic. Although I cannot deny the human tendency towards some form of "spirituality", from the simple sense of awe when observing nature and the universe to a deep Faith in the existence of Scientology's lord Xenu, I reject the notion that this somehow validates the idea that the spirit world actually exists. I appreciate the vacuum some people experience faced with the thought of a life without cosmic meaning. Personally, I think we choose to give meaning to our lives by our deliberate actions, decisions, and personal convictions. Our lives have obvious meaning to our offspring, and we all can play an important part in our towns and in our country. We can, on the other hand, also acquiesce to a meaning of life defined by someone else, like that of an organized Church; in that case, the meaning of life is whatever your church says it is.

Whatever need we have to "believe in something" varies from person to person and thus must be the result of individual and different personal variables. I do not have a problem with the concept inasmuch as spirituality refers to a sense of awe about the universe around us (this seems close to what Einstein was talking about). The universe *is* awe-inspiring and incredibly complex, maybe even beyond human comprehension. We humans are in effect self-conscious amoebas, ignorance is scary, and life is a white-water journey in uncharted territory. This alone is enough to make you want to ask for supernatural help. However, assuming for a moment that Lerner's observation is the complete answer to America's move towards the Right, answering the public's yearning for spirituality with a political movement is contrary to the basic idea of a secular democracy and not much different in my mind from what the Right is doing. The Left should not engage the Right on a debate about the best form of spirituality to win elections. Simply put, spirituality has no place in government.

We Americans take our jobs very seriously, a reflection of who we are as a people. However, we tend to forget that the economic machinery of the United States runs on the accumulation of capital, that of individuals and of private and public companies. Working in this system has obvious benefits, as our standard of living demonstrates, but also has downsides; worker depression and low self steem being well recognized since the time of the industrial revolution.

People in America today who find themselves unhappy with their work, people that feel it has become vulgar or debased, that it serves no "higher purpose" other than the accumulation of capital, have several options. It is unclear to me how staying in a self-described vulgar or debased job suddenly becomes better by believing in the existence of spirits; the job itself is not changed in any way. If one is suddenly feeling better, what has really changed? Could there be a potent psychological, as opposed to logical, component in this sudden feeling of elation? More to the point, looking for a reflection of one's own sense of "spirituality" in government is misguided. Government is not the place to look for spirituality, just the same as a job geared towards the accumulation of capital is not the place to look for spirituality. Government is simply the bureaucratic administration of institutions concerned with the running of the country and the making of secular laws to ensure the well-being of its citizens.

But, in a more general sense, what is the reality of the human situation on this planet?

The Four Noble Truths in Buddhism [4]

1. *Life is suffering;*
2. *Suffering is due to attachment;*
3. *Attachment can be overcome;*
4. *There is a path for accomplishing this.*

Even in the Christian tradition, life is described as a walk through a valley of tears.

If we look at the natural world for examples, life is not full of happiness for wild creatures. The simple fact that animals in some form of protective environment outlive those in the wild is testament that life in the wild for every organism in this planet is hard. Death and disease are routine; life in the wild is defined by the vital imperatives of constantly looking for food (which in most cases means killing and devouring other organisms), looking for shelter, and looking and finding a mate to procreate. In this state of affairs of living and dying, the dying is the easy part! [5] That is the way it is for every organism in this planet from the earthworm to the tiger and from seaweed to the oak tree. We humans are part of that continuum; we are creatures of this planet.

The best explanation our scientific method has come up with is that all life on this planet is the result of biochemical processes that evolved in ever increasing complexity over the span of many, many millions of years. The resulting organic species stayed alive and had offspring depending on their ability to adapt to their changing environments, and these became higher-level organisms by undergoing successful mutations and by a process of literally "survival of the fittest" where competition is the overriding rule. This is not a picture of eternal bliss. For most living things, life—staying alive—is a difficult enough process; dying is easier. A struggle to sustain life is what life is all about. "*We work to eat to get the strength to work to eat to get the strength to work*" wrote novelist John Dos Passos in 1934. To strive for *happiness* on top of that is a human expectation.

Happiness has relative elements associated with it depending on your particular status. For example, many Americans complain that medical insurance is too expensive; a common comment is that we are not happy with the costs of our medications. Whereas people in Africa would be completely ecstatic with even one tenth of the medical infrastructure we enjoy in this country. So the concept of happiness is subjective and quite possibly unique to the human species. Happiness in this life is not guaranteed for any species; it is indeed the exception rather than the rule. We humans experience unhappiness due to the nature of life itself, because of the inept and imperfect character of many of the social systems we ourselves created, and perhaps because of our own unrealistic expectations about what life is about. Inasmuch as we belong together with all other species living on this planet, we share the same characteristics of what being alive and trying to survive mean: toil, struggle, pain, and death. The concept of God can help only psychologically and here only marginally. Unless you actively do something about it, you still will be anchored to that vulgar and debased job even with all the Faith in the universe.

And yet, I think we humans are lucky in that we evolved enough intelligence to have the faculty of complex logical reasoning and to have discovered the scientific method. Our self-awareness, even though it perhaps brings in this sense of vacuum regarding life's purpose, also separates us from the other species on this planet. Our intelligence has allowed us in the span of something like 10,000 years (~500 generations) to move from living in caves and sharing pretty much the same living standards of wild grizzly bears, knowing no technology, no knowledge of even the most elemental facts about nature, and a lifespan of a few decades, to where we are today. Solving the food and shelter problems as successfully as we have has allowed us time to seriously ponder difficult philosophical questions about our own existence, and to try to understand our planet, our solar system, and our universe. Life expectancy has almost doubled in the last 100 years [6]. We taught ourselves how to extract metals from the ground and make tools, we have literally carved our present existence out of the raw earth. We taught ourselves everything we know; from agriculture, mathematics, chemistry, music, astronomy, physics, medicine to engineering. We invented democracy, we have ventured onto the moon and sent probes to other planets, and we are looking for other life forms out there in the big universal expanse. I think the development of all these technological, scientific, and social fields stands as a fantastic achievement for our species. And I would argue that humans are happier today than 100 years or even 50 years ago. It has not, however, been a road traveled entirely in a positive direction. We have been cruel to one another, we have had wars on a global scale, and there have been unspeakable crimes and injustices committed against each other, to say nothing of how we are treating the other species on this planet. Large economic disparities among nations persist, and these engender a sense of unfairness, despair and hopelessness among those that have fewer material acquisitions. Huge problems persist, and some days I feel pessimistic about our chances of solving them. We may yet kill ourselves and everything else on this planet. We do not need some God to accomplish this for us; but again, we may not. Today, I think we will be okay; life is good and I will try my best to make tomorrow the same as today; and that's all we can ultimately do.

From a personal perspective, if we can agree that the species is happier today than 100 years ago, that there are fewer injustices being committed and that there is real progress towards solving the world's problems (like for example the abolition of large scale slavery, advancement of the rights of women, large expansion of democratic institutions, universal education in countries that can afford it, the liberation of science from the grips of religious tyranny, development of science-based medicine, and many others), then we can agree that we have been on the right track more often than not and that we may yet find the maturity not to self-destruct. I cannot help feeling severely repulsed by those who rejoice whenever bloody military struggle heats up in the Middle East, thinking as they do that finally the Christian Rapture is at hand. In spite of this, I cannot help but feel optimistic about the future of our species given our ability to learn and our natural tendency to do whatever is required to endure one more day.

I think we are lucky to be alive, to be human, and to live in this day and age. All of us have truly won the cosmic lottery. Carl Sagan had it right when he pointed out that we are indeed made of stardust and that our story is more amazing than that in the biblical Genesis. I realize I speak from the perspective of a well-educated American. Had I been born in a poor developing country I might not feel exactly the same way about life. But even so, *as a species* I believe we have been zigzagging in a positive direction since the very beginning.

The concept of God undeniably brings solace to many; is it fair then to expose it as a fallacy? Is it unkind to strip humans of what for many is a major source of inspiration and spiritual comfort? There is a conundrum imbedded in these questions. If the concept of God brings happiness to people, and happiness is what ultimately we are all striving for, why not believe in God, even if is a fantasy, if it brings happiness? This problem is not dissimilar to the question of Santa Claus. It seems not only acceptable but even beneficial to allow children the fantasy of Santa; life is tough enough, and reality will come soon enough, so let them be happy. But almost anyone would agree that prolonging that fantasy for too long would have detrimental effects later on in life. The irrational belief in an unknowable and supernatural Santa (or God for that matter), brings with it several notions about life, the world, and the universe that are false, and more importantly, counterproductive and detrimental to our development. As a simple example, for centuries everyone in Europe was taught that the Earth was the center of the universe, and when Galileo came to dispute that claim in 1633, the Italian Inquisition imprisoned him. This historical fact is not only an example of unfair imprisonment, but also an example of how concepts derived from false beliefs in God have stood in the way of human development. Some historians have argued that had emperor Constantine not converted to Christianity in around 320 AD, we could have invented the Internet by the 1600's or even earlier. As it happened, humanity endured centuries of Christian superstition and ignorance during the middle or "dark" ages, remnants of which we still struggle with to this day. There is a heavy price to pay for living in a fantasy.

The well-known story of Galileo may seem to some an example of an obvious mistake, (even though Galileo was only "pardoned" in 1992) but is Galileo's example much different than the current Christian outrage against stem-cell research or Darwinian evolutionary theory? Is it not because of biblical interpretation or derived teachings that stem cell research is being curtailed? In this most industrialized and modern of countries some people today are against the teaching of evolutionary theory *precisely* because it goes against biblical scripture. Don't we want to know the truth about how species evolved? It seems that not much has changed since 1633; although at least no one is being imprisoned, or burned at the stake like Giordano Bruno. Even if the evolutionary theory is later deemed to be incorrect, we can rest assured that it will be by the scientific method that we determined so, not the Bible. The point being that by trying to curtail the teaching of scientific research because of religious concerns we are restraining our own discoveries and opportunities to learn more.

It is imperative that we recognize the connection between the concept of God and superstition and ignorance. This is why the concept of God, even if it brings some degree of happiness, must be exposed for the fallacy it is. Adults are by definition not children, they should care about the truth and should not attempt to prolong the fantasy because of a delusional sense of well-being. I am not proposing the abolition of organized religion, but I am advocating for a strict separation of religious teachings from interference with the workings of our government and in the instruction of the basic sciences. I am also trying to point out that God-derived spiritual happiness is but a mirage. Each of us is responsible for our own development and our own happiness. Many of us desperately seek and hold on to a mystical idea, one which deals with hope and love and of everything that is beautiful and "spiritual". This beckoning is so powerful that many will not only disregard every logical argument against it, but logical reasoning itself and will fight to the death to protect it. However, what is vital in this case is to critically examine the concept of God, and understand that it must be kept separate from government.

We must come to the realization that there are no guarantees of happiness in life. Despite working hard to achieve it, we might not succeed in fulfilling our expectations. This is just the way it is. Any notions of afterlife are but wishful hopes that bring with them a false sense of comfort confounded with a heavy penalty of superstition and the forced restriction on further knowledge. We must understand that just being alive is amazing enough, that ours is a tale of wonder of almost magical proportions. The concept of God is not a "white lie" like Santa; it is just a lie.

8

Religious Fanatics And Political Action.

Government affects people's lives in many important ways, and the mechanisms of organized political action (such as political parties) help determine the direction of governments. In autocratic, dictatorial, or tyrannical forms of government citizens enjoy few political freedoms and any action against the establishment is forbidden by law or actively discouraged by direct control of the forms of communication, by civilian repression, incarceration, or even the murder of any potentially effective opposition. In countries with tyrannical regimes citizens thus have little political mechanisms at their disposal to publicize their desires, let alone effect governmental change. Ironically, dictatorial regimes many times can be very effective in getting things done. It is easy to get things done if one does not allow open discourse or the dissemination of opposing views. For example, when the Chinese government wanted to build the Three Gorges Dam over the Yangtze River hundreds of thousands had to be evacuated. With little tools to influence policy, the affected Chinese citizens simply had to abandon their towns and homes and accept relocation to wherever their government said they had to go. The Chinese policy of one-child-per-couple is another example.

An argument could be made that since the well-being of the many overrides the well-being of the few, assuming for a second that a dictatorial government has the well-being of the many as its primary objective, such a regime may indeed be a good one; there being no real need for direct citizen interaction. Indeed an unpopular autocratic decree, such as one-child-per-couple, may be unavoidable when facing uncontrolled and unsustainable population growth. In any case, one key ingredient in any successful enterprise launched by a dictatorial government is that it is based on placing the well-being of the many first. History has shown, however, that in the long run dictatorships have a hard time placing the well-being of the many at the forefront of policy making. Instead the leadership becomes corrupt by greed and/or power and government resources are mobilized to work for the benefit of the very few top elite echelon of the population to the detriment of the people at large.

In democratic forms of government, the political agenda is set by elected officials chosen by the majority through a process of free elections. Important matters related to government policy are supposed to be articulated by leading members of the general populace and after active discussion, the general citizenry effectively decides what to do by voting into office the leaders that best reflect their opinions. The well-being of the many, or at least the electoral majority, is thus automatic. The critical key ingredient for this system of government to work is an educated citizenry, which comes in part from a crystal clear and unbiased presentation of the issues at hand. It should be apparent that if important issues are misrepresented or large numbers of the population are mislead, confused, or ignorant, the likelihood that correct decisions will be made is going to be slim.

Many factors affect the particular views of the electorate at any given time. In a country like America, which enjoys widely different views on almost any topic, policy course corrections are common. It could be argued that compared to a "benevolent" autocratic government, the American form represents the classic example of one step forward and two steps back. But history has shown that over the long run, an educated electorate will make correct decisions more often than otherwise. In order for the American system of government to work properly, by which I mean a pluralistic liberal secular democracy, it must rely on having a large percentage of responsible citizens. A responsible citizen is not only well informed and educated with regards to the very important issues at hand (where the media plays a vital role), but also must have a fundamental understanding of the principles that make the country function properly. Good citizenship also must include elements of tolerance and objectivity. These are essential ingredients simply because honest discourse of issues is vital for the system to work. Since no one has all the answers, compromise, tolerance and objective review of issues brought about by others is of paramount importance in a well functioning democracy. Wholesale outrage, condemnation, incarceration, or civil war cannot be the outcome of every disagreement. Indeed, in a country like America, made up of immigrants from all over the planet and thus representing an amalgam of many cultures and religions, a tolerant, liberal, and secular government is essential for it to function properly.

American evangelical fanatics, as part of the general citizenry, have equal rights in articulating their desires and electing into office whomever they feel best represents them. However, the question remains whether people that have a view of the world that is totally dominated by faith make good and effective citizens. Indeed, do fanatics of any kind make good citizens? Can we say religious fanatics are well informed? Tolerant? Or that they demonstrate objectivity on complicated issues?

> *Our job is to reclaim America for Christ, whatever the cost. As the vice regents of God, we are to exercise godly dominion and influence over our neighborhoods, our schools, our government, our literature and arts, our sports arenas, our entertainment media, our news media, our scientific endeavors—in short, over every aspect and institution of human society. D. James Kennedy* [1]
>
> *If we wish to adopt a form of Christianity consistent with the Bible, then we must seriously consider whether or not we are perhaps*

being deceived by our society and culture-and perhaps also by our own human selfishness-when we preach democracy as the panacea for all political problems. Aside from offering the citizen certain legal rights, most versions of democracy tell us we have the power and authority to claim for ourselves certain "inalienable rights", such as "life, liberty, and the pursuit of happiness". Yet this is one of the greatest political lies ever told! Christianity is a religion of the cross, a religion whose founder taught that true life comes only to those who are willing to die [see e.g., Mat. 10:38-39; 16:24; cf. 1 Cor. 15:31]. Among other things, this means Christians are called to give up all rights not just the basic right to "life", but also rights such as "liberty" and "the pursuit of happiness". For the Bible repeatedly says Christians are to be "slaves of Christ" [e.g., Eph. 6:6; Rom. 6:22] and are to endure all manner of suffering for the sake of a future glory [see e.g., Rom. 8:18; 1 Pet. 2:18-4:19]. How, then, can a Christian defend a political system which encourages its citizens to stand up and defend their "basic human rights"? . . . Democracy deceives people who deserve no rights into feeling they do deserve rights, and fools people into believing they are determining their own future. In fact, nowadays we are almost always at the mercy of deeper, more fundamental forces, which determine our ideas in ways more subtle than any political propaganda ever could. I am thinking here primarily of the media. Who controls the media? To a large extent the answer is advertisers-i.e., people with money, who are usually motivated by greed. And together these two forces, the media and the advertisers (as representatives of democracy and capitalism), shape what people think far more than most of us are aware [see e.g., E3:99-106; E4:19]. [Stephen Palmquist 2]

"Christians have an obligation, a mandate, a commission, a holy responsibility to reclaim the land for Jesus Christ—to have dominion in civil structures, just as in every other aspect of life and godliness. But it is dominion we are after. Not just a voice. It is dominion we are after. Not just influence. It is dominion we are after. Not just equal time. It is dominion we are after. World conquest. That's what Christ has commissioned us to accomplish." [George Grant, former executive director of D. James Kennedy's influential Coral Ridge Ministries, wrote in his book "The Changing of the Guard"]

"While it is true that the United States of America was founded on the sacred principle of religious freedom for all, that liberty was never intended to exalt other religions to the level that Christianity holds in

our country's heritage . . . Our founders expected that Christianity—
and no other religion—would receive support from the government as
long as that support did not violate peoples' consciences and their right
to worship. They would have found utterly incredible the idea that
all religions, including paganism, be treated with equal deference."
[Family Research Council]

Militant religious fanatics bent on political action, from Osama bin Laden to Pat Robertson and Jerry Falwell, argue for a regime change to an inflexible spiritual idea that only a small number of people can be privy to. Obviously, a form of government based on a religious idea cannot be democratic; not everyone can be allowed to talk to or receive instructions from God, or be allowed to interpret sacred scripture as a means to implement government policy. That is why in every theocracy there is some closed supreme council of religious leaders that set or ensure government policy follows religious doctrine; we see that in Iran at present and in the former Taliban regime in Afghanistan. In addition, an argument could be made that any political movement focused on implementing one particular view of the "will of God" cannot be amenable to compromise, tolerant of other points of view, or enjoy objectivity. On the contrary, in such a political system anything that may appear to go against a narrowly defined religious dogma is bound to be intolerant of any competing ideas, its policy would be dominated by various degrees of bigotry, prejudice, and repression of anything not aligned with the main religious thought. The degree to which some of the current fundamentalist Christian leaders express devotion to their particular idea of Jesus, and the militancy with which they seem to be willing to impose their views on others does not suggest they possess open minds or that they understand the nature of the American democracy. On the contrary, their propaganda and the degree of vitriol to which they subject anyone who stands in their way is reminiscent of Nazi leaders of the 1930s. In fact, Mel White, a former speech and book ghost writer for many of the most prominent fundamentalist Christians—thus someone with first hand knowledge of their objectives, tactics, and methods, makes a compelling argument that Falwell, Robertson, and others, rather than being Christian leaders in the Jesus tradition, are nothing more than modern-day Fascists. [3]

> *"You say you're supposed to be nice to the Episcopalians and the Presbyterians and the Methodists, and this and that and the other thing. Nonsense! I don't have to be nice to the spirit of the Antichrist."*
> *Pat Robertson* [4]
>
> *"My feeling as a Christian points me to my Lord and Savior as a fighter. It points me to the man who once in loneliness, surrounded by a few followers, recognized these Jews for what they were and summoned men to fight against them and who, God truth! was the greatest not as a sufferer but as a fighter . . . . And if there is anything which could demonstrate that we are acting rightly it is the distress that daily grows. For as a Christian I have also a duty to my own people."*
> *Aldolf Hitler* [5]

Democracy is not just about holding elections. We've witnessed elections in places with repressive governments like Cuba, Iran, and North Korea. I would argue that inasmuch as religious political action works towards undercutting the basic premises of a true democracy, such as the open discussion of all ideas, tolerance for other points of view without fear of recrimination, acceptance of the rights of others, rejection of bigotry and discrimination, to the degree that these democratic cornerstones are set aside and replaced with the blind worship of one metaphysical, mystical and repressive belief, such a movement represents nothing more than a particular form of a terrorist movement.

Consider the following exchange between Jerry Falwell and Pat Robertson after the events of September 11th [6]:

> *FALWELL:*   *I agree totally with you that the Lord has protected us so wonderfully these 225 years. And since 1812, this is the first time that we've been attacked on our soil and by far the worst results. And I fear, as*

Donald Rumsfeld, the Secretary of Defense, said yesterday, that this is only the beginning. And with biological warfare available to these monsters—the Husseins, the Bin Ladens, the Arafats—what we saw on Tuesday, as terrible as it is, could be miniscule if, in fact—if, in fact—God continues to lift the curtain and allow the enemies of America to give us probably what we deserve.

ROBERTSON: *Jerry, that's my feeling. I think we've just seen the antechamber to terror. We haven't even begun to see what they can do to the major population*

FALWELL: *The ACLU's got to take a lot of blame for this*

ROBERTSON: *Well, yes.*

FALWELL: *And I know that I'll hear from them for this. But, throwing God out successfully with the help of the federal court system, throwing God out of the public square, out of the schools. The abortionists have got to bear some burden for this because God will not be mocked. And when we destroy 40 million little innocent babies, we make God mad. I really believe that the pagans, and the abortionists, and the feminists, and the gays and the lesbians who are actively trying to make that an alternative lifestyle, the ACLU, People For the American Way—all of them who have tried to secularize America—I point the finger in their face and say: "You helped this happen."*

ROBERTSON: *Well, I totally concur, and the problem is we have adopted that agenda at the highest levels of our government. And so we're responsible as a free society for what the top people do, and, the top people, of course, is the court system.*

FALWELL: *Pat, did you notice yesterday the ACLU and all the Christ-haters, People For the American Way, NOW, etc. were totally disregarded by the Democrats and the Republicans in both houses of Congress as they went out on the steps and called out on to God in prayer and sang "God Bless America" and said "let the ACLU be hanged". In*

> *other words, when the nation is on its knees, the*
> *only normal and natural and spiritual thing to do*
> *is what we ought to be doing all the time—calling*
> *upon God.*

ROBERTSON: Amen.

At the time of national confusion after September 11th, Falwell and Robertson were quick to blame all those they disagree with for the terrorist act. Do these gentlemen sound like true supporters of democratic values as presented herein? Are their beliefs as expressed above representative of tolerance and openness to the ideas of others? Can we call their attack on others rational? Can we get a sense that these two men know what democratic values are? What sorts of values are expressed in views such as those above? Do we want people like these dominating or heavily influencing our government?

A form of government strictly aligned with a specific religious idea, intolerant of any other and deriving its laws and regulations based on religious dogma is at par with an autocratic dictatorship rather than a democracy. Again, we have examples currently in Iran and previously in the Taliban-dominated Afghanistan of just such a system of government. Indeed, the model we have been presented of godly institutions, and God's management style, is not democratic. We cannot expect Heaven to be a democracy. Are those who speak of implementing the "will of God" on Earth truly working to enhance democracy?

Of course, political realities in America are such that a full-blown Taliban-style theocracy is not probable. There is a spectrum of possibilities regarding what would constitute implementing the "will of God" by political action, from having the words "In God we Trust" on currency to forcing women to wear clothing from head to toe and executing "infidels" in soccer stadiums. But I would argue that the more our government moves to some form of narrowly defined "Christian values" the less supportive of democratic values it becomes.

*Theocracy: The term **theocracy** is commonly used to describe a form of government in which a religion or Faith plays the dominant role. Properly speaking, it refers to a form of government in which the organs of the religious sphere replace or dominate the organs of the political sphere. In the most common usage of the term theocracy, some civil rulers are leaders of the dominant religion (e.g., the Byzantine Emperor as head of the Church); governmental policies are either identical with, or strongly influenced by, the principles of a religion, and typically, the government claims to rule on behalf of God or a higher power, as specified by the local religion.* [7]

Below are some of the positions adopted in the platform of the Texas GOP which is heavily influenced by the Christian right [8]:

1. The Republican Party of Texas affirms that the United States of America is a Christian nation.
2. Our Party pledges to exert its influence to restore the original intent of the First Amendment of the United States Constitution and dispel the myth of the separation of Church and State.
3. The platform supports using tax dollars to fund Faith-based social programs and calls for allowing religious organizations to address vital issues of the day without losing tax-exempt status.
4. The platform condemns homosexuality, supports criminalizing sexual relations between consenting adults of the same sex and calls on Congress to withhold jurisdiction from the federal courts from cases involving sodomy.

I would argue that these provisions are more attuned to a theocracy than a democracy. I would argue that a government built on these principles would not be characterized by equal opportunities for the expression of ideas free from government censure and repression. I do not get a sense that a government based on those principles would be amenable to individual civil liberties. Taken to its inevitable conclusion, I could foresee that some panel of selected religious leaders would have to decide "moral values" for the rest of us.

Some valiant Christian militant might argue that since Christ is love, a Christian-based theocracy that ensures salvation of its citizens' souls in afterlife also ensures the well-being of the many in this life. In the course of human affairs we have witnessed political action based on religious principles promoting the well-being of the many become nothing more than instruments of repression and torture. The Spanish Inquisition comes to mind.

> *"There is no such thing as separation of church and state in the Constitution. It is a lie of the Left and we are not going to take it anymore." Pat Robertson* [9]

The truth is that people of faith that explain every important issue through the myopic perspective of biblical interpretation and "prophecy" live on the fringes of reality. People of faith that believe God, demons, or angels intercede and interfere in the daily doings of governments and other humans are not really "strong in their faith", they are *delusional*. I would argue that such people not only do not make good citizens, they are dangerous to the health of a democracy. Any strong political influence of such radical ideologues is dangerous to the health of the basic democratic principles of the United States. The government of this country needs to be *secular* if it is to be committed to respect *all* religious ideas, even the wackiest ones. As such, no single religious perspective can be allowed to become the dominant one. There must be complete separation of church and state, and government policies must be divorced from all types of religious-derived "morality". As has been argued here, the underlying principles of our government must be based on respect for personal civil rights and freedom to enhance life, liberty and the pursuit of happiness.

"When the government puts its imprimatur on a particular religion it conveys a message of exclusion to all those who do not adhere to the favored beliefs. A government cannot be premised on the belief that all persons are created equal when it asserts that God prefers some." Supreme Court Justice Blackmun. [10]

Unless the majority decides that we do indeed want to remake America into a fundamentalist Christian theocracy. A Christian Iran, with someone like Pat Robertson, or someone they can strongly influence, sitting on the White House.

It is interesting to ponder on this scenario. Say for example that 51% of the electorate would choose, in full recognition of what they are doing, to convert the United States into a full blown theocracy, a Christian Iran with someone like the late Jerry Falwell as President and eventually a majority of Christian scholars a la Pat Robertson in the Supreme Court. I would argue that not only would that constitute a very different country from what we have at present, but a complete opposition to what the Founding Fathers had in mind; but as they say—"majority rules". One could foresee that one would have to be an evangelical Christian to be elected to Congress, homosexuality would be severely punished, women would have to revert to their more "traditional" roles, the political agenda would have to be Christian first, and then serve the public second. One could envision a complete re-writing of biology books, and perhaps other scientific disciplines. Non-Christian books, or those criticizing Jesus or Christianity would be at the very least severely criticized, if not censured or outlawed. One can see that a theocracy is thus a form of dictatorship. It is arguable whether such a political system would be reversible by some future election. You see, even though it is theoretically possible to elect a theocracy in free elections (although I don't think this has happened often), the way back from a theocracy seems less certain. Like other forms of dictatorial regimes, history has shown that theocracy is a one-way street; once there, the most common way back is through civil war.

The Christian Right is not, to my knowledge, openly advocating for a Christian theocracy, although if you pay attention to the picture they paint of what they would like America to be, a theocracy is precisely what it looks like. They are, consciously or not, doing it through the established political parties. Their agenda is being portrayed as a call to a moral higher ground—going back to some basic moral principles; a moral ground which they define. It may seem like a good idea, the proper thing to do actually, to demand rectitude and a reflection of the popular code of behavior from the policies of our elected government. I do not have a problem with that specifically; however, the link to a very narrowly defined Christian morality is the problem. If we accept that acting morally is to behave out of concern for people's suffering and with respect to the rights of others to enjoy this life as they see fit as long as it does not infringe on the right of others, then we can dispense with a lot of Christian nonsense regarding morality. Homosexuals are not immoral as a result of their sexual preference. Research on stem-cells is not immoral as it causes no suffering to any real person. Adult women that consciously elect to terminate their pregnancy with an abortion are not acting immorally when they are making a mindful decision about what is best for them. Who gave the evangelical Christians the monopoly on morality?

An effective government, by which I mean the bureaucratic administration of civilian laws and the implementation of national and foreign policies, does not require any type of religious observance. We have at present strong democracies where the majority of their population declare themselves to be either atheists or agnostics. In fact, a strong religious influence may cloud the President's and Congress' judgment on specific issues. Whatever beliefs we may hold regarding God, we must come to the conclusion that God is better dealt with in His particular church, and the public administration of civil laws and regulations must be secular in nature. We can impose on ourselves additional rules and regulations based on what our Rabbi, Minister, or Priest tells us God wants, if we so choose—but God must be kept out of a democratic government if it wants to be free of repression. Thus, a theocracy has to be repressive to survive. The concept of God as an active participant in setting government policy is incompatible with democracy.

9

A Personal Conclusion.

The fact that nearly half of the American Population apparently believes [literal biblical interpretations], purely on the basis of religious dogma, should be considered a moral and intellectual emergency. Sam Harris in Letter to a Christian Nation.

When it comes to the current concepts of God, what has happened to us, particularly in the West, is quite easy to understand. For millennia the concept of God has been with us; spirits everywhere accompanying us in our dangerous hike through life on this planet. At the time of Jesus Christ there were literally thousands of Gods roaming the different corners of the Earth. The Jewish God was just one of them, and just like other Gods before, He presumably had a son, Jesus. The marketing by Peter and others of Jesus' death at the cross however (assuming for a second this actually did take place, an issue which is ultimately irrelevant), launched a political and religious movement that took off with a success that was simply unimaginable at the time. But this success was not due to "supernatural" reasons, or because of any strength in theological arguments. Much to the contrary, the historic record indicates that Christianity became dominant, and their promulgators the dominant elite, essentially due to the work of an influential few, and strictly by socio-political forces: conversion of kings, wars, repression, and indoctrination. For most humans the change from whatever God they were worshiping to a

Christian one was academic as the seed of belief in some form of deity had already been culturally implanted millennia before, so the process became a matter of "conversion". Faith comes naturally to humans. Reality is too unsettling, too uncertain, too scary, and in a human condition characterized by a combination of imagination, ignorance (or inappropriate levels of knowledge) and superstition, the belief in the existence of some supernatural God is simply a logical conclusion for most people. Besides, numbers do matter (as any marketing expert will tell you), and there are strong elements of group psychology in the spread of Christianity. After the Roman emperor Constantine became a Christian, for all practical purposes resistance was futile, not that many complained. One may argue that just as kingdoms were being consolidated into ever-increasing larger ones, on our long road to making countries, the same was happening to religious thought.

So we've always had gods, and probably always will. Historic political forces resulted in Christianity being the dominant religion in the West and in the United States. In the *Start Trek* episode when all the galactic species get together for the formation of the *United Federation of Planets*, if something of the sort were in store for our future, ours would not be the species characterized by the use of logic. Ours will be the species that always talks about some supreme spirit. Ours will be the mystical and "spiritual" species praying for enlightened answers from the heavens. As I have presented here, the invention of the concept of God came in handy early on as a quick explanation to primal questions surrounding death, and other perplexing natural phenomena. It also contributed to the formation of moral codes of behavior, which in turn helped in securing peaceful tribal coexistence, and thus our very survival. The psychological component of the fatherly figure/guidance counselor model of God cannot be overlooked either. Our present concepts of God are the end result of historic and political forces, not revelation and holiness. However, the concept of God has outlived its usefulness and indeed may at present be the conduit of our own demise. The irrational element associated with any implementation of "God's will", when connected to a focused political movement either from Al-Quaida or the Moral Majority, makes it imperative that we bring up for discussion the rationality of the belief in the illusory universal creator in all its forms. It may be impolite, but we cannot afford political correctness on this issue for much longer.

Some may protest placement of the late Jerry Falwell and Osama bin Laden in the same sentence. My point is that these two individuals represent points in a continuum. Falwell and other American fundamentalists like him do not resort to fostering the armed terrorist struggle Osama bin Laden is sponsoring simply because they do not have to. They can achieve their political objectives the way it is done in the west, which we can agree is a more civilized way of doing these things. That they live and speak their mind in a secular democracy ensures a peaceful outlet for the expression of their ideas. But neither Mr. Robertson nor Mr. Bin Laden are working to enhance a pluralistic liberal and secular society; far from it. Their objective is to implement their own versions of the "will of God" by political action. If Mr. Robertson and his followers had been born in Saudi Arabia, or Palestine, is it really that difficult to imagine them picking up an AK-47 in the name of their God?

> "I want you to just let a wave of intolerance wash over you. I want you to let a wave of hatred wash over you. Yes, hate is good . . . Our goal is a Christian nation. We have a Biblical duty, we are called by God, to conquer this country. We don't want equal time. We don't want pluralism." Randal Terry [1]
>
> "Just like what Nazi Germany did to the Jews, so liberal America is now doing to the evangelical Christians. It's no different. It is the same thing. It is happening all over again. It is the Democratic Congress, the liberal-based media and the homosexuals who want to destroy the Christians. Wholesale abuse and discrimination and the worst bigotry directed toward any group in America today. More terrible than anything suffered by any minority in history." [2]

The problem is that faith in any concept of God is an invitation to irrational behavior and to illogical ideas of morality, and we cannot afford to ignore the consequences of ignoring critical reasoning.

> . . . people of Faith tend to argue that it is not Faith itself but man's baser nature that inspires such violence. But I take it to be self-evident that ordinary people cannot be moved to burn genial old scholars alive for blaspheming the Koran, or celebrate the violent death of their children, unless they believe some improbable things about the nature of the universe. [Sam Harris, 3].

If we accept that this life is the only one we'll ever have, and we accept that there is no logical reason to believe there is an afterlife, or that humans aren't any different than trees, or fish, or any other organism on this planet when it comes to what happens after we die, then our life becomes **precious!** If we accept that life is precious and unique we can agree we all should work together to protect and enhance it for everyone. We must see that we do not need to be good to one another because of any celestial mandate but because if we are not, with no decent standards of behavior and fair government, chaos and anarchy are inevitable. We then see that we do not need some God to deduce the logic of moral and ethical behavior, so what is left for God then? The idea that some supreme being created us so that we would kill each other over how to best worship Him is preposterous and absurd. There is no special mission that explains human existence any more than there is some special mission for the existence of elephants. Therefore, it makes perfect sense to make *Life, Liberty and the pursuit of Happiness* our prime objective. If there is no outside reason why we are on this planet, and no life after death, then making the most of living on this planet is what we ought to be working towards. But we need to make fair rules for our self-government. At this time in our collective history, our rules cannot be based on antiquated concepts of celestial mandates that foster irrational regulations towards each other (i.e. laws against gays, women, embryonic cells, or others with different ideas of celestial creation), they must be based on fair rules of engagement that support the idea that we all have the right to *Life, Liberty and the pursuit of Happiness* as individually defined, and as long as it does not infringe on others. This is why it is irrational and wrong to make laws or establish government policy based on religious ideas. It is wrong for Afghanistan, Iraq, Israel, and particularly the United States. We must collectively get rid of this stagnant mental loop of the concept of God, at least inasmuch as it influences government policy in our country.

As pointed out elsewhere, ours is not a country founded on "Christian values." This much was made clear in the US Treaty of Tripoli signed by George Washington and many of the founding fathers, who knew something about the values this country was founded on. The Founding Fathers were not "conservatives"; in fact they probably were some of the most progressive and politically liberal humans of their time.

> ***Article 11 of the Treaty of Tripoli of 1797.*** *As the Government of the United States of America is not, in any sense, founded on the Christian religion; as it has in itself no character of enmity against the laws, religion, or tranquility, of Mussulmen; and, as the said States never entered into any war, or act of hostility against any Mahometan nation, it is declared by the parties, that no pretext arising from religious opinions, shall ever produce an interruption of the harmony existing between the two countries.*

Ultimately, when it comes to the question of God, it may prove too much to ask for a humanity that spans the gamut of technological development and even the most elementary knowledge of science to abandon a way of thinking that has been institutionally and culturally sustained for millennia. Perhaps the gaps are too wide and competing philosophical concepts too fragmented to expect consensus or even a balanced discussion regarding the concept of God. Perhaps the fact that there are such wide gaps in technological development and elemental science education explains some of the current divide between the East and the West. But in America, this turn towards Christian fundamentalism in government is a failure of citizenship. It is a failure of citizenship because we have the basic governmental structure that attempts to guarantee *Life, Liberty and the pursuit of Happiness* for everyone and we are about to let it turn into a fundamental evangelical theocracy. This is not the work of the informed majority of the public, it is the work of a focused, fanatical, and relentless minority combined with the general apathy and confusion of the rest. Even if it were the work of a conscientious majority, in creating a Christian theocracy, we would destroy everything the founding fathers worked so hard to achieve and many others since have fought hard to protect. It is a failure of citizenship because scientists and philosophers have failed to add their voices to the discussion in defense of rational thought and to explain the scientific method and the basics of logical thinking. It will be a failure of citizenship if ultimately we end up turning back the clock to the dark ages.

> *It is not the functioning of our government to keep the citizen from falling into error; it is the function of the citizen to keep the government from falling into error.* [US Supreme Court Justice R.H. Jackson 1950]
>
> *In every government on earth is some trace of human weakness, some germ of corruption and degeneracy, which cunning will discover and wickedness insensibly open, cultivate and improve. Every government degenerates when trusted to the rules of the people alone. The people themselves therefore are its only safe depositories. And to render even them safe, their minds must be improved* [Thomas Jefferson, 4]

We must see that inasmuch as religion brings happiness, solace, peace of mind, and hope to those who seek it, it's everyone's right to hold whatever personal beliefs on afterlife one might desire. From the heaven of Jesus Christ, to Heavens Gate's paradise UFO behind comet Halley-Bopp, to preparing to handle lord Xenu. But we must all understand that there isn't any generally accepted "true" belief, that we all do not agree on the concept of God, that in fact belief in the concept of God is cemented on faith and as such rests fundamentally on personal choice and personal conviction. For these reasons it is imperative that ideas of God-derived morality be extracted from a societal structure like government that is supposed to work for *everyone* and is supposed to foster the pursuit of life, liberty and happiness. This is not a "majority rules" type of issue because it is fundamental to the workings of our country. Strict secularism is non-negotiable. It has to be or we would indeed be creating a different country.

In America, no one should be forced to become a Christian if one does not want to. A secular democracy does not force any Christian to become an atheist. The termination of an unwanted pregnancy by an abortion is not forced upon anyone that does not want one; adoption is still a perfectly workable and available alternative. If you do not feel sexual attraction to others of your same sex, why should you care about those that do? No one is forcing anyone to become a homosexual by allowing homosexuals to marry, nor is homosexuality being fostered by marriage between same-sex couples. If two humans love each other and want to establish a form of public social contract based on their mutual love and would like to ensure that civilian legal mechanics work in their favor, why should anyone stand in their way? No one else's marriage is being threatened in any way. Intelligent Design is not biology, it is philosophy, teach it in philosophy class. The Ten Commandments are part of the Christian dogma and as such have no place in a courtroom designed to serve everyone regardless of their religion; put them in a Christian church. We have to be careful that "Christian values" are not a clever euphemism for intolerance, the promulgation of ignorance, and bigotry.

The machinery of political demagoguery is being spun furiously by Christian elements that are bent on obtaining more political power to change America to a theocracy; whether they realize it or not. If we disagree with the notion that specific religious elements should have a strong influence in our government, we must reject this attempt. God must stay in His church, whichever one you want it to be. But our government is not a church, and that is how it should remain.

References

1—Introduction—Attack on Secularism

1. Taken from: *http://www.religioustolerance.org/dc_jones.htm*

> *The People's Temple—This was a Christian destructive, doomsday cult founded and led by James Warren Jones (1931-1978). Jim Jones held degrees from Indiana University and Butler University. He was not a Fundamentalist pastor as many reports in the media and the anti-cult movement claim. He belonged to a mainline Christian denomination, having been ordained in the Christian Church/Disciples of Christ. (At the time of his ordination, the DoC allowed a local congregation to select and ordain a minister on their own. However, ordinations conducted without denominational endorsement were not considered valid within the rest of the church.)*
>
> *The Peoples Temple was initially structured as an inter-racial mission for the sick, homeless and jobless. He assembled a large following of over 900 members in Indianapolis IN during the 1950's. "He preached a 'social gospel' of human freedom, equality, and love, which required helping the least and the lowliest of society's members. Later on, however, this gospel became explicitly socialistic, or communistic in Jones' own view, and the hypocrisy of white Christianity was ridiculed while 'apostolic socialism' was preached."It was an interracial congregation—almost unheard of in Indiana at the time. When a government investigation began into his cures for cancer, heart disease and arthritis, he decided to move the group to Ukiah in Northern California. He preached the imminent end of the world in a nuclear war; Ukiah was judged to be as safe as any when war broke out. They*

later moved to San Francisco and Los Angeles. After an expose during the mid 1970's in the magazine New West raised suspicions of illegal activities within the Temple, he moved some of the Temple membership to Jonestown, Guyana. The Temple had leased almost 4,000 acres of dense jungle from the government. They established an agricultural cooperative there, called the "Peoples Temple Agricultural Project." They raised animals for food, and assorted tropical fruits and vegetables for consumption and sale.

Jones developed a belief called Translation in which he and his followers would all die together, and would move to another planet for a life of bliss. Mass suicides were practiced in which his followers pretended to drink poison and fell to the ground.

During the late 1970's, Jones had been abusing prescription drugs and appears to have become increasingly paranoid. Rumors of human rights abuses circulated. As in most high-intensity religious groups, there was a considerable flow of people joining and leaving the group. Tim Stoen, the Temple attorney and right-hand man to Jones left to form Concerned Relatives who claimed that Jonestown was being run like a concentration camp, and that people were being held there against their will. This motivated Leo Ryan, a Congressman, to visit Jonestown in 1978-NOV for a personal inspection. At first, the visit went well. Later, on NOV-18, about 16 Temple members decided that they wanted to leave Jonestown with the visitors. This came as quite a blow to both Jones and the rest of the project. While Ryan and the others were waiting at Port Kiatuma airfield, the local airstrip, some heavily armed members of the Temple's security guards arrived and started shooting. Congressman Ryan and four others were killed; three were members of the press; the other was a person from Jonestown who wanted to leave. 11 were wounded. Fearing retribution, the project members discuss their options. They reach a consensus to commit group suicide. 914 died: 638 adults and 276 children. Some sources say 911 died. Most appear to have committed suicide by drinking a grape drink laced with cyanide and a number of sedatives, including liquid Valium, Penegram and chloral hydrate. Some sources say it was Kool-Aid; others say FlaVor-Aid®. Other victims appear to have been murdered by poison injection. The Guyanese coroner said that hundreds of bodies showed needle marks, indicating foul play. Still other victims were shot. A very few fled into the jungle and survived. The bodies were in a state of extensive decay when the authorities arrived. There was no time to conduct a thorough investigation. TV station KTVU in

San Francisco CA has a collection of photographs of the "Peoples temple Agricultural Project." Some are quite disturbing. Unfortunately, their web site implies that all of the dead committed suicide.

The Peoples Temple organization did not survive the mass suicide/murder in Guyana. Their former headquarters building in San Francisco was demolished by the Loma Prieta earthquake of 1989.

2. See: http://www.pbs.org/now/politics/217/perspectives.html. Kenyn M. Cureton, is a Vice President at the Executive Committee of the Southern Baptist Convention.

3. http://www.geocities.com/capitolhill/7027/quotes.html. Marion Gordon "Pat" Robertson (born March 22, 1930) is a televangelist from the United States. He is the founder of numerous organizations and corporations, including the American Center for Law and Justice (ACLJ), Christian Broadcasting Network (CBN), the Christian Coalition, Flying Hospital, International Family Entertainment, Operation Blessing International Relief and Development Corporation, and Regent University. He is the host of *The 700 Club,* a Christian TV program airing on channels throughout the United States and on CBN affiliates worldwide. He is opposed to abortion and gay rights. Robertson is a supporter of the Republican Party and campaigned unsuccessfully to become the party's nominee in the 1988 presidential election. He is a Southern Baptist and was active as an ordained minister with that denomination for many years, but holds to a Charismatic theology not traditionally common among Southern Baptists. As a result of his seeking political office, he no longer serves in an official role for any church. Despite this, his media and financial resources make him a recognized and influential, albeit controversial, public voice for conservative Christianity in the United States.

4. http://www.usvetdsp.com/osam_qts.htm

5. Harold Lee "Hal" Lindsey (born 1929) is an American evangelist and Christian writer. A graduate of the Dallas Theological Seminary, a prominent Christian Zionist and dispensationalist, he expresses this

theology in his writings. In *The Late, Great Planet Earth*, Lindsey wrote that he had concluded, since there was no apparent mention of the United States in the books of Daniel or Revelation, that the USA would no longer be a major player on the geo-political stage by the time the tribulations of the end times arrived. Lindsey also predicted that the European Common Market, which preceded the European Community, was destined (according to Biblical prophecy) to become a "United States of Europe", which in turn he says is destined to become a revived Roman Empire ruled by the Antichrist. See: http://mediamatters.org/items/200509130004.

6. Intro to Hal Linday's—Great Global Deception—The Antichrist waits in the Wings.

7. See: http://www.pbs.org/now/politics/217/perspectives.html. Michelle Goldberg is a senior political reporter for Salon.com and Author of "Kingdom Coming.

8. *http://www.geocities.com/capitolhill/7027/quotes.html*

9. http://www.adherents.com/largecom/com_atheist.html

2—Believe In God, But Which One?

1. http://www.mediamatters.org/items/200509130004

2. CNN.com Friday, January 6, 2006; Posted: 5:33 a.m. EST (10:33 GMT). See http://www.cnn.com/2006/US/01/05/robertson.sharon/

3. Pat Robertson; Washington Post November 11, 2005.

4. CNN.com September 14, 2001 Posted: 2:55 AM EDT (0655 GMT). See http://archives.cnn.com/2001/US/09/14/Falwell.apology/

5. Charles R. Monroe, World Religions—An Introduction (New York: Prometheus Books, 1995).

6.   Sam Harris, The End of Faith. Religion, Terror, and The Future of Reason (New York: W. W. Norton & Company, 2005 ed.) p. 37.

7.   Pedro Calderon de la Barca—Life is a Dream. Translated by Edeward Fitzgerald, New York: P.F. Collier & Son Company, 1909—14. Actual Spanish text, which is quite beautiful, is as follows:

> Sueña el rey que es rey, y vive
> con este engaño mandando,
> disponiendo y gobernando;
> y este aplauso, que recibe
> prestado, en el viento escribe,
> y en cenizas le convierte
> la muerte, ¡desdicha fuerte!
> ¿Que hay quien intente reinar,
> viendo que ha de despertar
> en el sueño de la muerte!
> Sueña el rico en su riqueza,
> que más cuidados le ofrece;
> sueña el pobre que padece
> su miseria y su pobreza;
> sueña el que a medrar empieza,
> sueña el que afana y pretende,
> sueña el que agravia y ofende,
> y en el mundo, en conclusión,
> todos sueñan lo que son,
> aunque ninguno lo entiende.
> Yo sueño que estoy aquí
> de estas prisiones cargado,
> y soñé que en otro estado
> más lisonjero me vi.
> ¿Qué es la vida? Un frenesí.
> ¿Qué es la vida? Una ilusión,
> una sombra, una ficción,
> y el mayor bien es pequeño;
> que toda la vida es sueño,

8. Chet Raymo—Skeptics and True Believers (Walker Publishing Co. 1998).

9. Taken from an article by Ann Druyan in Skeptical Inquirer magazine, November 2003. See: http://www.csicop.org/si/2003-11/ann-druyan.html

10. Augustine—Sermo LII vi 6.

11. See: http://www.rapturechrist.com/rapture2.htm

3—Science and This Thing Called Faith

1. Kant, I, 'Denying Knowledge to Make Room for Faith' in Helm P, Oxford Readers: Faith and Reason, Oxford University Press: Oxford, 1999 p.203.

2. Astronaut Scott Carpenter, Graduate Education Monitor, U. of Colorado, 1987.

3. Michael Behe—http://www.actionbioscience.org/evolution/nhmag.html

4. Ayn Rand, Introduction to Objectivist Epistemology (New York: Penguin Books, Expanded 2nd Ed 1990).

5. George H. Smith, Atheism The Case Against God (Buffalo: Prometheus Books, 1979) p. 104.

6. Robert Nadeau and Menas Kafatos, The Non-Local Universe, (New York: Oxford University Press, 1999.

7. Albert Einstein, *The World as I See It*, London 1955. p. 131.

8. Definition taken freely from Wikipedia. http://en.wikipedia.org/wiki/Pantheism.

9. *The New York Times*, April 19, 1955.

10. *Albert Einstein: The Human Side*, Princeton University Press.

11. Albert Einstein, *Ideas and Opinions*, New York 1954, pg. 46.

12. Denis Brian, *Einstein, A Life*, New York 1996. p. 277f.

13. E.G. Larson, L. Witham; Nature, Vol. **394**, No. 6691, p. 313 (1998)

14. http://www.nwcreation.net/atheism.html#anchorgalluppolls

15. George H. Smith, Atheism The Case Against God (Buffalo: Prometheus Books, 1979) p. 105.

16. Sam Harris, The End of Faith. Religion, Terror, and The Future of Reason (New York: W. W. Norton & Company, 2005 ed.) p.66.

17. George H. Smith, Atheism The Case Against God (Buffalo: Prometheus Books, 1979) p. 124.

18. George H. Smith, Atheism The Case Against God (Buffalo: Prometheus Books, 1979) p. 90.

19. George H. Smith, Atheism The Case Against God (Buffalo: Prometheus Books, 1979) p. 123.

20. See: http://query.nytimes.com/gst/fullpage.html?sec=health&res=9506 E4DA153AF93BA15750C0A961958260

4—Jesus As Proof

1. Oscar Cullmann La Prière dans le Nouveau Testament, 2e édition, Cerf 1996. See also:
http://www.tempemasjid.com/maurice/10sources.htm
http://members.iinet.net.au/~quentinj/Christianity/Gospel-Timeline.html

2. http://www.thenazareneway.com/new_testament_biblical_inconsistencies.htm

3. Frederick Conybeare—The Origins of Christianity.

4. The Catholic Encyclopedia. See:
http://www.newadvent.org/cathen/11744a.htm

5. The Catholic Encyclopedia. See:
http://www.newadvent.org/summa/4046.htm

6. The Catholic Encyclopedia. See:
http://www.newadvent.org/summa/4048.htm

5—*What About Pascal*

1. http://www.iep.utm.edu/p/pasc-wag.htm
2. Taken from 1. The best known defense of Pascal is Lycan & Schlesinger 1989; for responses see Amico 1994 and Saka 2001. A good sourcebook is Jordan 1994a (below).

Amico, Robert (1994) "Pascal's wager revisited", International Studies in Philosophy 26:1-11.

Armour-Garb, Bradley (1999) "Betting on God", Religious Studies 35:119-38.

Byl, John (1994) "On Pascal's wager and infinite utilities", Faith & Philosophy 11:467-73.

Clifford, William (1879) "The ethics of belief", Lectures & Essays, Macmillan.

Duff, Anthony (1986) "Pascal's wager and infinite utilities", Analysis 46:107-09.

Franklin, James (1998) "Two caricatures, I: Pascal's wager", International Journal for Philosophy of Religion 44:115-19.

Hacking, Ian (1972) "The logic of Pascal's wager", reprinted in Jordan 1994a.

James, William (1897) "The will to believe", reprinted in The Will to Believe and Other Essays, Dover.

Jordan, Jeff (1991) "The many-gods objection and Pascal's wager", International Philosophical Quarterly 31:309-17.

a. —(1993) "Pascal's wager and the problem of infinite utilities", Faith & Philosophy 10:49-59.

b. —, editor (1994a) Gambling on God, Lanham MD: Rowman & Littlefield.

c. —(1994b) "The many-gods objection", in Jordan 1994a; a restatement of Jordan 1991.

Lycan, William & George Schlesinger (1989) "You bet your life", in Reason & Responsibility, 7th edition (ed. Joel Feinberg, Belmont CA: Wadsworth). Also in the 8th, 9th, 10th editions; in Philosophy and the Human Condition, 2d edition (ed. Tom Beauchamp et al., Englewood Cliffs NJ: Prentice Hall, 1989); and in Contemporary Perspectives on Religious Epistemology (ed. Douglas Geivet & Brendan Sweetmar, Oxford, 1993). See also Schlesinger 1994.

Mackie, J.L. (1982) The Miracle of Theism, Oxford, pp. 200-03. Martin, Michael (1975) "On four critiques of Pascal's wager", Sophia 14:1-11.

—(1990) Atheism, Philadelphia: Temple University Press, pp. 229-38.

Mougin, Gregory & Elliott Sober (1994) "Betting on Pascal's wager", Nous 28:382-95.

Nicholl, Larimore (1978) "Pascal's wager: the bet if off", Philosophy & Phenomenological Research 39:274-80.

Pascal, Blaise (composed in 1600s, first published in 1800s) Pensees, section 343; translated & reprinted by Penguin and many others.

Rescher, Nicholas (1985) Pascal's Wager, University of Notre Dame Press.

Saka, Paul (2001) "Pascal's wager and the many gods objection", Religious Studies 37:321-41.

Schlesinger, George (1994) "A central theistic argument", in Jordan 1994a; a restatement of Lycan & Schlesinger 1989.

3. Sorensen, Roy (1994) "Infinite decision theory", in Jordan 1994a. http://newsweek.washingtonpost.com/onfaith/sam_harris/2007/04/the_cost_of_betting_on_faith.html.
4. Smith's Wager—How to Defend Atheism. A speech given to the Society of Separationists in 1976. see: http://www.infidels.org/library/modern/george_smith/defending.html

6—Religion and Morality

1. Texas Observer, October 7, 2005. Mary Ann Markarian is a gospel singer. She is the wife of Gilbert Markarian, a business entrepreneur and National Director of the Full Gospel Business Men's Fellowship International. Mary Ann has appeared on the Trinity Broadcasting Network with Paul Crouch, the Daystar Network with Marcus & Joni Lamb, and with Pat Robertson/Ben Kinchlow on the 700 Club.

2.   Sultan M. Munadi; The Reach of War Trial; Mental Health Evaluation May Derail Case Against Afghan Convert to Christianity. The New York Times, March 27, 2006.

3.   Sam Harris, The End of Faith. Religion, Terror, and The Future of Reason (New York: W. W. Norton & Company, 2005 ed.) p. 170.

4.   ibid. p.186.

5.   George H. Smith, Atheism The Case Against God (Buffalo: Prometheus Books, 1979) p.285.

6.   http://en.wikipedia.org/wiki/Secularism#Secular_ethics

7.   C. F. Volney, Ruins or Meditations on the Revolutions of Empires and the Law of Nature (New York: Kessinger Publishing, 1997).

7—A Beautiful Life

1.   Michael Lerner, The Left Hand of God, Talking Back Our Country from the Religious Right, HarperCollins 2006.

2.   The American Heritage College Dictionary 3rd Ed. Houghton Mifflin Co. Boston, 1993.

3.   http://en.wikipedia.org/wiki/Spirituality

4.   Dr. C. George Boeree—*http://www.ship.edu/%7Ecgboeree/buddhawise.html*

5.   Paraphrased from an episode of HBO's TV series *Carnivale*.

6.   http://www.cdc.gov/nchs/data/hus/hus05.pdf#027

8—Religious Fanatics and Political Action

1.   D. James Kennedy, Pastor of Coral Ridge Ministries,

2.   Stephen Palmquist, Biblical Theocracy: A vision of the biblical foundations for a Christian political philosophy (Hong Kong: Philopsychy Press, 1993). **Note:** In private correspondence Dr. Palmquist

explained his position on democracy as follows: *'The political philosophy my approach has most similarity to is libertarianism, or even more accurately (though only in an ideal sense) religiously-moderated anarchy. As I say in [Biblical Theocracy], democracy may well be the best NON-religious option available today as a "realistic" way of implementing the ideal I present in my book. My objection is only to those religious enthusiasts who promote democracy as THE (one and only) ANSWER presented in the Bible.'* He agrees with me however that: *'Theocracy as typically understood, like the political engagement promoted by most "American evangelical fanatics", is anything BUT a promotion of individual freedom and a call for responsible engagement in tolerant political relationship with those who believe differently.*

3. Mel White; Religion Gone Bad—The Hidden Dangers of the Christian Right. Penguin Books, 375 Hudson St. New York, NY 10014, 2006. See Chapter 7. See also: *www.ratical.org/ratville/CAH/fasci14chars.pdf* and *www.oldamericancentury.org/14pts.htm*

4. Rob Boston, *Pat Robertson, the Most Dangerous Man in America?*, Prometheus Books, 1996, p. 149.

5. Adolf Hitler, speech of 12 April 1922. Norman H. Baynes ed. *The Speeches of Adolf Hitler April 1922-August 1939.* Vol. 1. Oxford University Press, 1942.

6. *http://www.truthorfiction.com/rumors/f/falwell-robertson-wtc.htm.* Both Falwell and Robertson have apologized for the statements made during the interview.

7. Taken from: http://en.wikipedia.org/wiki/Theocracy

8. The Anatomy of Power, Texas and The Religious Right in 2006. A Report from the Texas Freedom Network Education Fund. See: http://www.tfn.org/files/fck/SORR%2006%20ReportWEB.pdf

9. Pat Robertson, November 1993 during an address to the American Center for Law and Justice.

10. Supreme Court Justice Harry A. Blackmun in the Lee v. Weisman ruling, 1992.

9—A Personal Conclusion

1. Randall Terry, Founder of Operation Rescue, The News-Sentinel, Fort Wayne, Indiana, 8-16-93

2. Pat Robertson, 1993 interview with Molly Ivins.

3. Sam Harris, The End of Faith. Religion, Terror, and The Future of Reason (New York: W. W. Norton & Company, 2005 ed.) p. 31.

4. Thomas Jefferson from *Notes on Virginia*.

Appendix

Gods!

See: http://www.lowchensaustralia.com/names/gods.htm

Common Nordic Gods:

Aesir	Principal race of gods in Norse mythology.
Andhrimnir	The cook of the Aesir.
Angrboda	Goddess and wife of Loki
Astrild	Goddess of love.
Atla	Water goddess.
Audhumla	The primeval cow, formed from the melting ice.
Balder	Fairest of the gods
Beyla	The servant of Freyr.
Borghild	Goddess of the evening mist or moon, she slays the sun each evening.
Bragi	God of poets and the patron of all skaldi (poets) in Norse culture.
Brono	The son of Balder. He is the god of daylight.
Bylgia	Water goddess.
Dagur	The personification of day, he drives the day chariot across the sky.

Disen	A group of goddess in old Norse mythology. Called the "Dis of the Vanir".
Eir	Goddess of healing and shamanic healers, companion of the goddess Frigg
Elli	Goddess of old age.
Fenrir	Also known as Fenris. The great wolf, child of Loki and Angrboda
Forseti	God of justice who settles court disputes in his gilded hall.
Freya	Goddess of love, beauty and sensuality.
Freyr	God of fertility, sun and rain.
Frigg	Wife of Odin and the goddess of marriage and fertility.
Gefion	Goddess of agriculture and the plough.
Gerd	The wife of Freyr and a goddess of fertility. She is the personification of the fertile soil.
Heimdall	God of light and protection.
Hel	The goddess of death and ruler of the realm of the dead.
Hermod	The messenger of the gods. Often equated to the Greek god Hermes.
Hod	Blind god of darkness and winter.
Holler	God of disease and destruction.
Idun	Goddess of the spring, eternal youth and the keeper of the golden apples
Jord	Goddess of the primitive and unpopulated earth.
Jormungand	The Midgard Serpent
Kari	Leader of the storm giants.
Kvasir	The wisest of the Vanir gods.

Laga	Goddess of wells and springs.
Lofn	Goddess of forbidden love, who blesses all illicit love affairs.
Loki	Trickster god of the Norse, concerned with thievery, magic and fire.
Magni	Son of Thor and god of brute strength.
Mani	God of the moon and brother of the sun goddess Sol.
Miming	Minor forest god.
Mimir	Wisest god of the Aesir, sent in a hostage trade to the rival Vanir gods.
Modi	God of battle wrath, he was the leader of the berserkers.
Njord	God of the sea, wind and fire. He bestows good fortune to those on the sea.
Norns	The triple goddesses of fate and destiny.
Nott	Goddess of night who mans the night-charion in it's track through the sky.
Odin	The chief god of the Aesir and most important of the Norse deities.
Ran	Goddess of storms and the drowned dead.
Saga	Goddess of poetry and history.
Sif	Wife of Thor, and possibly an ancient fertility goddess.
Sjofn	Goddess of love, passion and marital harmony.
Skadi	A frost giant and goddess of winter.
Sleipnir	The eight-legged horse of Odin
Sol	Goddess of the sun, who guides the sun-chariot through the sky.
Syn	Goddess of watchfulness and truth.

Thor	Thunder-god and the protector of men and gods.
Tyr	The original god of war in the Germanic culture
Ull	God of justice and duelling, archery and skiing.
Vali	Son of Odin, and the god born to avenge the death of Balder.
Valkyries	The battle-maidens, who choose the best warriors
Vanir	A group of fertility and nature gods
Var	Goddess of contracts and marriage agreements
Vidar	Son of Odin and the god of silence and vengeance.

Common Roman Gods:

Apollo	Roman God of Sun, Music, Poetry, Prophecy, and Healing
Bacchus	Roman God of Wine
Bellona	Roman Goddess of War
Ceres	Roman Goddess of Corn
Cupid	Roman God of Love
Diana	Roman Goddess of Fertility, Hunting, and the Moon
Faunus	Roman God of Prophecy
Flora	Roman Goddess of Flowers
Janus	Roman God of Gates and Doors
Juno	Roman Goddess of Marriage and Women
Jupiter	Supreme King of the Roman Gods
Lares	Roman God of Household and Estate
Libintia	Roman Goddess of Funerals
Maia	Roman Goddess of Growth and Increase

Mars	Roman God of War
Mercury	Roman messenger God and Commerce God
Minerva	Roman Goddess of Wisdom, Arts, and Trade
Mithras	Roman God of Sun and Light
Neptune	Roman God of the Sea
Ops	Roman Goddess of Fertility
Pales	Roman Goddess of Flocks and Sheppard's
Pluto	Roman God on the Underworld
Pomona	Roman Goddess of Fruit Trees and Fruit
Proserpine	Roman Goddess of the Underworld
Saturn	Roman God of Seeds and Harvest
Venus	Roman Goddess of Beauty and Love
Vertumnus	Roman God of Seasons
Vesta	Roman Goddess of the Hearth
Vulcan	Roman God of Fire

Classic Greek Gods:

Aphrodite	Greek Goddess of Love and Beauty
Apollo	Greek God of Music
Ares	Greek God of War
Artemis	Greek Goddess of the Night and the Hunt. Protector of Women
Athena	Goddess of Wisdom, War, Art, Industry, Justice, and Skill
Demeter	Greek Goddess of Corn, Grain, and the Harvest
Dionysus	Greek God of Wine, Agriculture, and Fertility of Nature
Hades	Ruler of the Underworld
Helios	Greek God of the Sun

Hephaestus	Greek God of Smiths and Fire
Hera	Great Queen of Mount Olympus. Goddess of Marriage and Birth
Hermes	Greek God of Riches, Trade, and Luck
Hestia	Greek Goddess of Hearth Fire and Domestic Life
Persephone	Goddess of the Underworld
Poseidon	Greek God of the Sea
Selene	Goddess of the Moon
Zeus	Ruler of all the Greek Gods. God of the Light and the Sky

Native Celtic Gods:

Airmid	Celtic Goddess of Healing, Medicine, and Spring. Brings the dead back to life.
Artio	Celtic Goddess of the Wild
Balor	Celtic Goddess with a venomous eye. Good on the battlefield
Branwen	Celtic Goddess of Love and Beauty
Camalus	Celtic God of the Sky and War
Cerunnos	Celtic God of Fertility, Life, Animals, Wealth, and the Underworld
Cyhiraeth	Celtic Goddess of Streams
Druantia	Queen of the Druids. Protector of Trees, Knowledge, Creativity, Passion, Sex, & Fertility
Giobhniu	Celtic God of Weaponry
Lugh	Celtic God of Druids, Carpentry, and Mason
Llyr	Celtic God of Waters and Sea
Maeve	Celtic Goddess of Earth, Fertility, and War

Manannan	Celtic God of Sailors and Merchants
Margawse	Celtic Goddess of Mothers
Mebd	Celtic Goddess of War and Drinking
Mider	Celtic God of the Underworld
Morrigan	Celtic Goddess of War, Death, Ravens, Fertility, the Dark Goddess, and Fate
Nemain	Celtic Goddess of Panic and War

Native Irish Gods:

Aine	Irish Celtic Goddess of Love and Fertility
Angus Og	Irish Celtic God of Beauty
Anu	Irish Celtic Goddess of Manifestation Magick, Moon, Air, Fertility, and Prosperity
Babd Catha	Irish Celtic Goddess of War
Bel	Irish Celtic God of Fire and Sun
Bran	Irish Celtic God of Health
Brighid	Irish Celtic Goddess of Fire and Water. One of the triple Goddesses
Bris	Irish Celtic God of Fertility and Agriculture
Dagda	Irish Celtic God of the Earth, and father God. Leader of the Tuatha de Danaan
Danu	Irish Celtic Goddess of Rivers, Water, Wells, Prosperity, Magick, and Wisdom
Diancecht	Irish Celtic God of Healing and Medicine
Flidais	Irish Celtic Goddess of Nature, Forests, Woodlands, and Wild Things
Labraid	Irish Celtic God of the Underworld
Macha	Irish Celtic Goddess of Beauty and Brightness
Niamh	Irish Celtic Goddess of Beauty and Brightness

Native Welsh:

Arawn	Welsh Celtic God of the Underworld, Terror, Revenge, and War
Arianrhod	Welsh Celtic Goddess of Air, Reincarnation, Full Moons, Karma, and Retribution
Amaethon	Welsh Celtic God of Husbandry, Agriculture, and Luck
Blodeuwedd	Welsh Celtic Goddess of Wisdom, Moon Mysteries, and Initiations.
Cerridwen	Welsh Celtic Goddess of the Moon, Poetry, Music, Luck, Earth, Death, Fertility,
Dewi	Welsh Celtic God of Dragons
Don	Welsh Celtic Goddess of the Heavens, Air, Sea, and the Moon.
Dylan	Welsh Celtic God of the SEA
Elaine	Welsh Celtic Maiden Goddess
Gwydion	Welsh Celtic God of Warriors and Magic
Gwynn Ap Nudd	Welsh Celtic God of the Underworld
Math Ap Mathowny	Welsh Celtic God of Magic, Sorcery, and Enchantment
Myrrdin	Welsh Celtic God of Druids, Magic, and Sorcery. Also known as Merlin

Slavic Gods:

Belobog	White God; master of light, source of good, happiness and luck
Berstuk	the evil god of the forest in Wendish Mythology
Crnobog	(The Black God), the god of night and darkness in Slavic Mythology

Dazbog	Sun God
Flins	the god of death in Wendish Mythology
Hors	the Slavic god of the winter sun
Jarilo	Slavic god of spring fertility
Juthrbog	the god of the moon (Wendish Mythology)
Karewit	the protector of the town of Korzenica (Wendish Mythology)
Lada	the goddess of harmony, merriment, youth, love and beauty
Lado	the god of m4arriage, mirth, pleasure and general happiness
Marowit	the god of nightmares (Wendish Mythology)
Perun	the highest god of the pantheon (Slavic Mythology)
Podaga	the weather god and the god of fishing, hunting and farming. (Wendish Mythology)
Porewit	the god of law, order and judgement. (Wendish Mythology)
Radegast	the Slavic god of hospitality, fertility, and crops
Rod	initial original god—progenitor of deities
Siebog	the male god of love and marriage
Simargl	Slavic god of fire, hearth
Stribog	the god and spirit of the winds, sky and air
Svarog	the Slavic god and spirit of fire
Svetovid	the Polabian deity of war, fertility and abundance.
Triglav	a complex god or gods in Slavic mytholog
Veles	a Slavic god, deity of: cattle, commerce, music, divination and the underworld
Zirnitra	a black Slavic dragon and the god of sorcery (Wendish Mythology)

Japanese Gods:

Aizen-Myoo   God of love, worshipped by prostitutes, landlords, singers and musicians.

Aji-Suki-Taka-Hi-Kone   God of thunder.

Ama-No-Minaka-Nushi   'Divine Lord of the Middle Heavens' and god of the Pole Star.

Amaterasu   Shinto goddess of the sun and the leader of the Shinto pantheon.

Amatsu Mikaboshi   God of evil, his name means "August Star of Heaven".

Amatsu-Kami   Gods of heaven who live 'above' the earthly plain. Heavenly and eternal.

Ama-Tsu-Mara   Shinto god of smiths. He is pictured as a Cyclops.

Ame-No-Mi-Kumari   Shinto water goddess.

Ame-No-Wakahiko   God sent to rule the earth. Killed by the sky god Takami-Musubi.

Amida   God of death, to whom the devout turned at the moment of their death.

Am-No-Tanabata-Hime   Goddess of weavers.

Baku   A good spirit, known as the 'eater of dreams'.

Benten   Goddess of love, the arts, wisdom, poetry, good fortune and water.

Benzai-Ten   See Benten.

Bimbogami   God of poverty. Rituals are performed to get rid of him.

Binzuru-Sonja   God of curing illness and good vision.

Bishamon   God of war, justice and protector of the law. He is one of the Shichi Fukujin

Bosatsu   Manifestation of the Buddha in the past, present or future. See bodhisattva.

Butsu   See Buddha.

Chien-shin	A kami which is related to particular geographical area
Chimata-no-kami	Go of crossroads, highways and footpaths. He was originally a phallic god
Chup-Kamui	Sun goddess of the Ainu. She was originally the moon goddess
Daibosatsu	The Great bodhisattva or the Buddha in his last incarnation.
Daikoku	God of wealth, the soil and patron of farmers.
Dainichi	Buddhist personification of purity and wisdom.
Dosojin	God of roads.
Dozoku-shin	Ancestral kami of a dozoku, or clan.
Ebisu	God of the wealth of the sea, he is the patron god of fishermen and fishing.
Ekibiogami	God of plagues and epidemics.
Emma-o	Japanese Buddhist god of the underworld. He is the judge of the dead
Fudo	God of fire and wisdom, god of Astrology.
Fujin	Shinto god of the wind. Seen as a terrifying dark demon in a leopard skin
Fukurokuju	Shinto god of wisdom, luck and prosperity.
Funadama	The boat-spirit, goddess who protects and helps mariners and fishermen.
Futsu-Nushi-no-Kami	God of fire and lightning, a war god and general of Ameratsu.
Gama	God of longevity.
Gekka-o	God of marriage. He binds the feet of lovers with a red silken cord.
Hachiman	God of war and agriculture, divine protector of the Japanese people.

Haniyasu-hiko	God of the earth.
Haniyasu-hime	Goddess of the earth.
Haya-Ji	God of the whirlwind.
Hiruko	God of the morning sun. Guards the health of little children.
Hoso-no-Kami	God of smallpox.
Hotei	God of happiness, laughter and the wisdom of being content.
Ida-Ten	Buddhist god of the law and of monasteries. A handsome young man.
Ika-Zuchi-no-Kami	Group of even Shinto demons who reside in the Underworld.
Iki-Ryo	The spirit of anger and envy which harms.
Inari	Both a male and female deity, god/goddess of rice and agriculture.
Isora	God of the seashore.
Izanagi	Primordial god of the sky and the creator of everything good and right.
Izanami	Primordial goddess of the earth and darkness.
Jinushigami	Minor deity who watches over a town or plot of land.
Jizo	Japanese Buddha of great compassion.
Juichimen	Buddhist god of mercy.
Jurojin	Shinto god of longevity and a happy old age. One of the Shichi Fukujin
Kagutsuchi	Japanese god of fire.
Kamado-gami	Gods of the hearth.
Kami-kaze	God of wind, storms and viscous cold weather.
Kaminari	Goddess of thunder, the Thunder Queen and the Heavenly Noise.
Kanayama-hiko	God of metals.

Kanayama-hime	Goddess of metals.
Kawa-no-Kami	God of rivers. Although rivers had their own god, ruler of all rivers.
Kenro-Ji-Jin	God of earth.
Kishi-Bojin	Goddess of children and childbirth
Kishijoten	Goddess of luck and beauty
Kishimo-jin	Buddhist goddess of compassion and protectress of children.
Kojin	Ancient tree deity and goddess of the kitchen. She lives in an enoki tree.
Ko-no-Hana	The Blossom Princess, she is the goddess of spring
Koshin	God of the roads.
Koya-no-Myoin	God of the sacred Mount Koya.
Kukunochi-no-Kami	Shinto god of the trees.
Kuni-Toko-tachi	Earth deity who lives in Mt. Fuji.
Kura-Okami	God of rain and snow.
Marisha-Ten	Queen of heaven, goddess of the light, sun and moon.
Mawaya-no-kami	Kami, or deity of the toilet
Miro	Japanese name for Maitreya.
Miyazu-Hime	Goddess of royalty.
Monju-Bosatsu	Japanese Buddhist bosatsu of wisdom and knowledge.
Musubi-no-Kami	God of love and marriage. Appears as a handsome young lover.
Nai-no-Kami	God of earthquakes.
Naka-Yama-Tsu-Mi	God of mountain slopes.
Nikko-Bosatsu	Buddhist god of sunshine and good health.
Ninigi-no-mikoto	Rice god and ancestral god of the Japanese imperial family.
Nominosukune	God of wrestling.

Nyorai	Japanese name for all of the Buddha's appearances.
Oanomochi	God of the crater of Mt. Fuji.
Ohonamochi	A god of the earth.
Oho-Yama	The great mountain god.
Okuni-Nushi	God of magic and medicine, ruler of the unseen things and the spirit world.
Owatatsumi	God of the sea.
Oyamatsumi	A god of the mountains
Raiden	God of thunder and lightning
Ryo-Wo	God of the sea. known as the Dragon King
Sae-no-Kami	A group of kami, or deities, who guard the roads of Japan.
Sambo-kojin	God of the kitchen. Pictured with three faces and two pairs of hands.
Sarutahiko Ohkami	God of crossroads, paths and overcoming obstacles.
Sengen	See Ko-no-Hana.
Shaka	The silent sage, the wisest and first appearance of Buddha on earth.
Shichi Fujukin	Gods of Luck: Benten, Bishamon, Daikoku, Ebisu, Fukurokuju, Hotei
Shinda	Ainu fertility god of the island of Hokkaido.
Shine-Tsu-Hiko	God of the wind, he fills the space between heaven and earth.
Shoden	See Ganesha.
Shoki	God of the afterlife and exorcism.
Suijin	Deity of the water.
Suitengu	Child god of the sea.
Sukuna-Biko	Dwarf god of healing, agriculture and hot springs.
Susanowa	God of the winds, storms, ocean and snakes in Shinto mythology.

Takami-Musubi	Primordial sky god and creator of living things in Shinto belief.
Takemikadzuchi	A thunder god.
Taki-Tsu-Hiko	God of rain.
Tatsuta-hime	Goddess of autumn.
Tenjin	God of learning, language and calligraphy. He taught humans to write.
Toyo-Uke-Bime	Goddess of earth, food and agriculture.
Toyouke-Omikami	Goddess of grain.
Tsuki-Yumi	God of the moon and brother of the sun goddess Ameratsu.
Uba	Spirit of the pine tree. Means 'old woman' or 'wet nurse'.
Uga-Jin	Serpent god of the waters and fertility of the earth.
Uga-no-Mitama	Goddess of agriculture.
Ukemochi	Goddess of fertility and food.
Uzume	Shinto goddess of joy and happiness.
Wakahiru-me	Goddess of the rising sun.
Wata-tsu-mi	God of the sea.
Yabune	Japanese house god.
Yama-no-kami	Goddess of the hunt, forest, agriculture and vegetation.
Yamato	The soul or spirit of Japan.
Yuki-Onna	The Snow Queen or goddess of winter.